GRE

Math Workbook

Abundant Exercises and Two Full-Length GRE Math Practice Tests

By

Michael Smith & Reza Nazari

GRE Math Workbook

Published in the United State of America By

The Math Notion

Web: www.MathNotion.com

Email: info@Mathnotion.com

GRE Math Workbook

GRE Math Workbook covers all Math topics you will ever need to prepare for the GRE Math test. This workbook contains the key areas of the GRE Math. It reviews the most important components of the GRE test. This workbook offers plenty of practice questions to challenge students for achieving the high score on their real GRE Math test. GRE Math Workbook is the ideal prep solution for anyone who wants to pass the GRE Math test. Not only does it provide abundant math exercises, but it also contains practice test questions as well as detailed explanations of each answer.

This Math workbook is filled with exercises and worksheets covering fundamental math, arithmetic, algebra, geometry, basic statistics, probability, and data analysis. Answers are provided for all math questions, and two full-length GRE Math tests with detailed answers and explanations can help you discover your weak areas for concentrated study. Here is comprehensive preparation for the GRE Math section, and a valuable learning tool for the GRE test takers who need to improve their knowledge of Mathematics and prepare for the GRE Math test.

Each chapter and topic of the book go into detail to cover all the content likely to appear on the GRE test. This completely revised edition reflects all the new types of math questions that will appear on the GRE.

Developed by experienced GRE Math teachers and authors for test takers trying to achieve a passing score on the GRE test, this comprehensive Math workbook includes:

- Over 2,000 revised Math questions to practice with

- Easy–to–follow activities

- Fun and interactive exercises that build confidence

- Topics are grouped by category, so you can easily focus on the topics you struggle on

- 2 Full-length and REAL GRE Math tests

- Detailed answers and explanations for the GRE Math practice tests

After completing this workbook, you will gain confidence, strong foundation, and adequate practice to ace the GRE Math test.

Get the help and confidence you need to be well prepared for the GRE Math test!

About the Author

Michael Smith has been a math instructor for over a decade now. He holds a master's degree in Management. Since 2006, Michael has devoted his time to both teaching and developing exceptional math learning materials. As a Math instructor and test prep expert, Michael has worked with thousands of students. He has used the feedback of his students to develop a unique study program that can be used by students to drastically improve their math score fast and effectively.

- GRE Math Workbook
- Accuplacer Math Workbook
- TSI Math Workbook
- SAT Math Workbook
- ACT Math Workbook
- Common Core Math Workbooks
- GED Math Workbook
- and many Math Education Workbooks…

As an experienced Math teacher, Mr. Smith employs a variety of formats to help students achieve their goals: He tutors online and in person, he teaches students in large groups, and he provides training materials and textbooks through his website and through Amazon.

You can contact Michael via email at:

info@Mathnotion.com

WWW.MathNotion.COM

... So Much More Online!

✓ FREE Math lessons

✓ More Math learning books!

✓ Mathematics Worksheets

✓ Online Math Tutors

Need a PDF version of this book?

Please visit www.MathNotion.com

Contents

Chapter 1:

Integer and Complex Numbers

Topics that you'll learn in this chapter:

➢ Rounding and Estimates

➢ Addition and Subtraction Integers

➢ Multiplication and Division Integers

➢ Arrange and ordering Integers and Numbers

➢ Comparing Integers, Order of Operations

➢ Mixed Integer Computations

➢ Integers and Absolute Value

➢ Adding and Subtracting Complex Numbers

➢ Multiplying and Dividing Complex Numbers

➢ Graphing Complex Numbers

➢ Rationalizing Imaginary Denominators

"Wherever there is number, there is beauty." –Proclus

Adding and Subtracting Integers

✏️ Find the sum.

1) $(-14) + (-5)$

2) $7 + (-21)$

3) $(-15) + 24$

4) $(-9) + 28$

5) $33 + (-14)$

6) $(-23) + (-4) + 3$

7) $3 + (-16) + (-20) + (-19)$

8) $(-28) + (-19) + 31 + 16$

9) $(-7) + (-11) + (27 - 19)$

10) $6 + (-20) + (35 - 24)$

11) $(+24) + (+32) + (-47)$

12) $41 + 17 + (-29)$

✏️ Find the difference.

13) $(-6) - (-32)$

14) $(-14) - (9)$

15) $(26) - (-8)$

16) $(42) - (7)$

17) $(-13) - (-7) - (19)$

18) $(64) - (-3) + (-6)$

19) $(7) - (4) - (-2)$

20) $(3) - (5) - (-14)$

21) $(24) - (3) - (-24)$

22) $(-37) - (-72)$

23) $(-11) - 24 + 32$

24) $32 - (-16) - (-13)$

Multiplying and Dividing Integers

✎ **Find each product.**

1) $(-7) \times (-4)$

2) 7×6

3) $(-3) \times 7 \times (-4)$

4) $3 \times (-7) \times (-7)$

5) $12 \times (-14)$

6) $20 \times (-6)$

7) 9×8

8) $(-5) \times (-13)$

9) $7 \times (-8) \times 3$

10) $8 \times (-1) \times 5$

11) $(-7) \times (-9)$

12) $(-12) \times (-11) \times 2$

✎ **Find each quotient.**

13) $56 \div 8$

14) $(-60) \div 4$

15) $(-72) \div (-8)$

16) $28 \div (-7)$

17) $38 \div (-2)$

18) $(-84) \div (-12)$

19) $37 \div (-1)$

20) $(-169) \div 13$

21) $81 \div 9$

22) $(-24) \div (-3)$

23) $(-6) \div (-1)$

24) $(-65) \div 5$

Arrange, Order, and Comparing Integers

✍ Order each set of integers from least to greatest.

1) $-12, -17, 12, -1, 1$ ___, ___, ___, ___, ___, ___

2) $11, -7, 5, -3, 2$ ___, ___, ___, ___, ___, ___

3) $25, -52, 19, 0, -22$ ___, ___, ___, ___, ___, ___

4) $31, -84, 0, -13, 47, -55$ ___, ___, ___, ___, ___, ___

5) $-45, 39, 21, -18, -51, 42$ ___, ___, ___, ___, ___, ___

6) $-17, -65, 71, -25, -51, -39$ ___, ___, ___, ___, ___, ___

✍ Order each set of integers from greatest to least.

7) $81, 5, 36, 19, 77, 24$ ___, ___, ___, ___, ___, ___

8) $-1, 7, -3, 4, -7$ ___, ___, ___, ___, ___, ___

9) $-47, 17, -17, 27, 37$ ___, ___, ___, ___, ___, ___

10) $-21, 19, -14, -17, 15$ ___, ___, ___, ___, ___, ___

11) $1, 0, -1, -2, 2, -3$ ___, ___, ___, ___, ___, ___

12) $-124, -91, 31, -28, -75, 19$ ___, ___, ___, ___, ___, ___

✎ Compare. Use >, =, <

1) 0 ____ 1

2) -12 ____ -17

3) 0 ____ -21

4) 41 ____ -56

5) -654 ____ -645

6) -42 ____ -48

7) -68 ____ -20

8) -86 ____ -106

9) -26 ____ (-26)

10) 425 ____ -425

Order of Operations

✎ Evaluate each expression.

1) $41 - (8 \times 3)$

2) $7 \times 6 - (\dfrac{16}{12 - (-4)})$

3) $32 - (4 \times (-2))$

4) $(6 \times 5) + (-3)$

5) $(\dfrac{(-2)+4}{(-1)+(-1)}) \times (-6)$

6) $(14 + (-2) - 3) \times 7 - 5$

7) $\dfrac{40}{3(9 - (-1)) - 10}$

8) $38 - (4 \times 6)$

9) $-43 + (4 \times 8)$

10) $((-12) + 18) \div (-2)$

11) $(-60 \div 3) \div (-12 - 8)$

12) $47 + (-8) \times (\dfrac{(-18)}{6})$

Integers and Absolute Value

✎ Write absolute value of each number.

1) 22

2) − 12

3) − 31

4) 0

5) 47

6) − 9

7) − 1

8) 37

9) -23

10) − 4

11) − 57

12) 19

13) − 15

14) − 55

✎ Evaluate.

15) $|-29| - |13| + 20$

16) $39 + |-15 - 42| - |3|$

17) $28 - |-47| - 61$

18) $|56| - |-18| + 19$

19) $|101| - |-38| - 20$

20) $|42| - |-68| + 70$

21) $|-87 + 73| + 15 - 9$

22) $|-6| + |-17|$

23) $|-9 + 5 - 2| + |6 + 6|$

24) $|-14| - |-23| - 5$

Adding and Subtracting Complex Numbers

✎ *Simplify.*

1) $-6 + (3i) + (-6 + 5i)$

2) $10 - (6i) + (5 - 12i)$

3) $-3 + (-5 - 6i) - 8$

4) $(-15 - 4i) + (12 + 6i)$

5) $(4 + 2i) + (9 + 3i)$

6) $(6 - 2i) + (3 + i)$

7) $3 + (4 - 4i)$

8) $(9 + 9i) + (6 + 5i)$

9) $(-4i) - (-6 + 2i)$

10) $(-12 + 2i) - (-10 - 10i)$

11) $(-12i) + (2 - 4i) + 8$

12) $(-10 - 8i) - (-8 - 2i)$

13) $(13i) - (15 + 3i)$

14) $(-2 + 4i) - (-6 - i)$

15) $(-3 + 15i) - (-5 + 5i)$

16) $(-12i) + (3 - 4i) + 5$

Multiplying and Dividing Complex Numbers

✎ *Simplify.*

1) $(2i)(-i)(2-5i)$

2) $(2-5i)(2-4i)$

3) $(-3+6i)(2+5i)$

4) $(5+3i)(5+8i)$

5) $(2+3i)^2$

6) $3(3i)-(2i)(-5+3i)$

7) $\dfrac{3+2i}{12+2i}$

8) $\dfrac{2-2i}{-3i}$

9) $\dfrac{2+6i}{-1+8i}$

10) $\dfrac{-5+i}{-7+i}$

11) $\dfrac{4+5i}{i}$

12) $\dfrac{-2i}{4-2i}$

13) $\dfrac{2}{-9i}$

14) $\dfrac{-2-6i}{4i}$

15) $\dfrac{9i}{3-i}$

16) $\dfrac{-1+3i}{-6-5i}$

17) $\dfrac{-2-4i}{-2+3i}$

18) $\dfrac{6+i}{2-7i}$

Graphing Complex Numbers

✎*Identify each complex number graphed.*

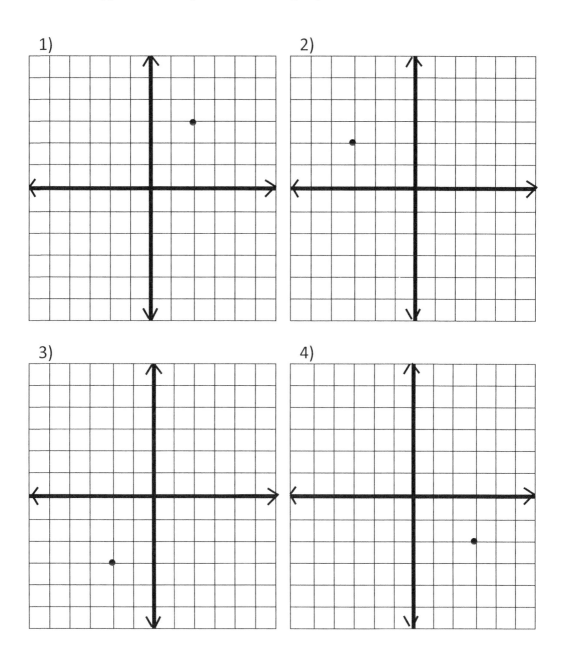

1)

2)

3)

4)

Rationalizing Imaginary Denominators

✎ *Simplify.*

1) $\dfrac{8-8i}{-4i}$

2) $\dfrac{2-10i}{-8i}$

3) $\dfrac{5+7i}{9i}$

4) $\dfrac{6i}{-1+2i}$

5) $\dfrac{7i}{-2-6i}$

6) $\dfrac{-10-5i}{-4+4i}$

7) $\dfrac{-2-6i}{6+8i}$

8) $\dfrac{-6-3i}{7-12i}$

9) $\dfrac{-1+i}{-7i}$

10) $\dfrac{-4-i}{i}$

11) $\dfrac{c}{ib}$

12) $\dfrac{-3-i}{6+4i}$

13) $\dfrac{-5+i}{-3i}$

14) $\dfrac{-8}{-i}$

15) $\dfrac{-4-i}{-1+4i}$

16) $\dfrac{-16-4i}{-4+4i}$

17) $\dfrac{8}{-6i}$

18) $\dfrac{-4i-1}{-1+3i}$

Answers of Worksheets – Chapter 1

Adding and Subtracting Integers

1) – 19	9) – 10	17) – 25
2) – 14	10) – 3	18) 61
3) 9	11) 9	19) 5
4) 19	12) 29	20) 12
5) 19	13) 26	21) 45
6) – 24	14) –23	22) 35
7) – 52	15) 34	23) –3
8) 0	16) 35	24) 61

Multiplying and Dividing Integers

1) 28	9) – 168	17) –19
2) 42	10) – 40	18) 7
3) 84	11) 63	19) –37
4) 147	12) 264	20) –13
5) – 168	13) 7	21) 9
6) – 120	14) – 15	22) 8
7) 72	15) 9	23) 6
8) 65	16) – 4	24) –13

Arrange and Order, Comparing Integers

1) – 17, – 12, – 1, 1, 12	7) 81, 77, 36, 24, 19, 5
2) – 7, – 3, 2, 5, 11	8) 7, 4, – 1, – 3, – 7
3) – 52, – 22, 0, 19, 25	9) 37, 27, 17, – 17, – 47
4) – 84, – 55, – 13, 0, 31, 47	10) 19, 15, – 14, – 17, –21
5) –51, –45, –18, 21, 39, 42	11) –3, –2, -1, 0,1,2
6) – 65, – 51, – 39, – 25, – 17, 71	12) 31, 19, –28, –75, –91, –124

Compare.

1) <	5) <	9) =
2) >	6) >	10) >
3) >	7) <	
4) >	8) >	

Order of Operations

1) 17	5) 6	9) −11
2) 41	6) 58	10) −3
3) 40	7) 2	11) 1
4) 27	8) 14	12) 71

Integers and Absolute Value

1) 22	9) 23	17) − 80
2) 12	10) 4	18) 57
3) 31	11) 57	19) 43
4) 0	12) 19	20) 44
5) 47	13) 15	21) 20
6) 9	14) 55	22) 23
7) 1	15) 36	23) 18
8) 37	16) 93	24) −14

Adding and Subtracting Complex Numbers

1) $-12 + 8i$	7) $7 - 4i$	13) $-15 + 10i$
2) $15 - 18i$	8) $15 + 14i$	14) $4 + 5i$
3) $-16 - 6i$	9) $6 - 6i$	15) $2 + 10i$
4) $-3 + 2i$	10) $-2 + 12i$	16) $8 - 16i$
5) $13 + 5i$	11) $10 - 16i$	
6) $9 - i$	12) $-2 - 6i$	

Multiplying and Dividing Complex Numbers

1) $4 - 10i$

2) $-16 - 18i$

3) $-36 - 3i$

4) $1 + 55i$

5) $-5 + 12i$

6) $6 + 19i$

7) $\frac{40+18i}{148}$

8) $\frac{2}{3} + \frac{2}{3}i$

9) $\frac{46}{65} - \frac{22}{65}i$

10) $\frac{18-i}{25}$

11) $-4i + 5$

12) $\frac{1}{5} - \frac{2}{5}i$

13) $\frac{2i}{9}$

14) $\frac{i-3}{2}$

15) $\frac{27i-9}{10}$

16) $-\frac{9}{61} - \frac{23i}{61}$

17) $-\frac{8}{13} + \frac{14i}{13}$

18) $\frac{5}{53} + \frac{44i}{53}$

Graphing Complex Numbers

1) $2+3i$

2) $-3+2i$

3) $-2-3i$

4) $3-2i$

Rationalizing Imaginary Denominators

1) $2i + 2$

2) $\frac{5+i}{4}$

3) $\frac{-7+5i}{9}$

4) $\frac{-6i+12}{5}$

5) $\frac{-7i-21}{20}$

6) $\frac{5+15i}{8}$

7) $\frac{-3-i}{5}$

8) $\frac{-6-93i}{193}$

9) $\frac{-i-1}{7}$

10) $4i - 1$

11) $-\frac{ic}{b}$

12) $\frac{-11+3i}{26}$

13) $\frac{-1-5i}{3}$

14) $-8i$

15) $0 + 1i$

16) $\frac{3+5i}{2}$

17) $\frac{4i}{3}$

18) $\frac{-11+7i}{10}$

Chapter 2: Fractions and Decimals

Topics that you'll learn in this chapter:

➢ Simplifying Fractions

➢ Adding and Subtracting Fractions, Mixed Numbers and Decimals

➢ Multiplying and Dividing Fractions, Mixed Numbers and Decimals

➢ Comparing and Rounding Decimals

➢ Converting Between Fractions, Decimals and Mixed Numbers

➢ Factoring Numbers, Greatest Common Factor, and Least Common Multiple

➢ Divisibility Rules

"A Man is like a fraction whose numerator is what he is and whose denominator is what he thinks of himself. The larger the denominator, the smaller the fraction." –Tolstoy

Simplifying Fractions

✍ **Simplify the fractions.**

1) $\dfrac{42}{62}$

2) $\dfrac{18}{24}$

3) $\dfrac{10}{15}$

4) $\dfrac{36}{48}$

5) $\dfrac{9}{27}$

6) $\dfrac{20}{80}$

7) $\dfrac{12}{27}$

8) $\dfrac{28}{56}$

9) $\dfrac{40}{100}$

10) $\dfrac{7}{63}$

11) $\dfrac{25}{45}$

12) $\dfrac{24}{32}$

13) $5\dfrac{35}{56}$

14) $2\dfrac{26}{32}$

15) $9\dfrac{5}{25}$

16) $3\dfrac{35}{56}$

17) $1\dfrac{52}{104}$

18) $4\dfrac{13}{65}$

19) $1\dfrac{45}{60}$

20) $\dfrac{54}{60}$

21) $7\dfrac{66}{132}$

Factoring Numbers

🖋 List all positive factors of each number.

1) 32

2) 26

3) 40

4) 96

5) 60

6) 28

7) 35

8) 64

9) 56

10) 75

11) 81

12) 48

🖋 List the prime factorization for each number.

13) 20

14) 65

15) 99

16) 42

17) 84

18) 30

19) 52

20) 105

21) 75

22) 48

23) 36

24) 31

25) 24

26) 54

Greatest Common Factor (GCF)

✎Find the GCF for each number pair.

1) 14, 28	7) 16, 12	13) 36, 42
2) 48, 36	8) 45, 60	14) 15, 90
3) 6, 18	9) 36, 72	15) 63, 84
4) 25, 15	10) 27, 63	16) 100,75
5) 52, 39	11) 64, 48	17) 26, 42
6) 57, 38	12) 80, 45	18) 93, 62

Least Common Multiple (LCM)

✎Find the LCM for each number pair.

1) 6, 9	7) 42, 63	13) 16, 32, 24
2) 25, 35	8) 21, 12	14) 15, 25, 35
3) 64, 48	9) 64, 44	15) 14, 8, 21
4) 12, 18	10) 15, 12	16) 5, 9, 7
5) 14, 21	11) 75, 6	17) 14, 6, 16
6) 45, 15	12) 20, 10, 40	18) 36, 60, 24

Divisibility Rules

✍ **Use the divisibility rules to find the factors of each number**

1) 24   2 3 4 5 6 7 8 9 10

2) 32   2 3 4 5 6 7 8 9 10

3) 16   2 3 4 5 6 7 8 9 10

4) 42   2 3 4 5 6 7 8 9 10

5) 28   2 3 4 5 6 7 8 9 10

6) 56   2 3 4 5 6 7 8 9 10

7) 48   2 3 4 5 6 7 8 9 10

8) 36   2 3 4 5 6 7 8 9 10

9) 81   2 3 4 5 6 7 8 9 10

10) 50   2 3 4 5 6 7 8 9 10

11) 63   2 3 4 5 6 7 8 9 10

12) 84   2 3 4 5 6 7 8 9 10

Adding and Subtracting Fractions

✎ **Add fractions.**

1) $\dfrac{1}{3} + \dfrac{1}{2}$

4) $\dfrac{5}{12} + \dfrac{1}{3}$

7) $\dfrac{2}{7} + \dfrac{5}{7}$

2) $\dfrac{2}{7} + \dfrac{2}{3}$

5) $\dfrac{3}{6} + \dfrac{1}{5}$

8) $\dfrac{5}{13} + \dfrac{2}{4}$

3) $\dfrac{3}{7} + \dfrac{4}{9}$

6) $\dfrac{3}{15} + \dfrac{2}{5}$

9) $\dfrac{16}{56} + \dfrac{3}{16}$

✎ **Subtract fractions.**

10) $\dfrac{3}{5} - \dfrac{1}{10}$

13) $\dfrac{1}{8} - \dfrac{1}{9}$

16) $\dfrac{2}{25} - \dfrac{1}{15}$

11) $\dfrac{5}{8} - \dfrac{2}{5}$

14) $\dfrac{3}{5} - \dfrac{5}{12}$

17) $\dfrac{3}{4} - \dfrac{13}{18}$

12) $\dfrac{5}{6} - \dfrac{2}{7}$

15) $\dfrac{5}{8} - \dfrac{5}{16}$

18) $\dfrac{8}{42} - \dfrac{7}{48}$

Multiplying and Dividing Fractions

✐ **Multiplying fractions. Then simplify.**

1) $\dfrac{2}{7} \times \dfrac{3}{8}$

2) $\dfrac{4}{25} \times \dfrac{5}{8}$

3) $\dfrac{9}{40} \times \dfrac{10}{27}$

4) $\dfrac{6}{13} \times \dfrac{26}{33}$

5) $\dfrac{9}{12} \times \dfrac{4}{5}$

6) $\dfrac{12}{17} \times \dfrac{3}{5}$

7) $\dfrac{28}{115} \times 0$

8) $\dfrac{8}{9} \times \dfrac{9}{8}$

9) $\dfrac{14}{45} \times \dfrac{15}{28}$

✐ **Dividing fractions.**

10) $0 \div \dfrac{1}{10}$

11) $\dfrac{5}{12} \div 5$

12) $\dfrac{6}{11} \div \dfrac{3}{4}$

13) $\dfrac{21}{32} \div \dfrac{7}{8}$

14) $\dfrac{4}{19} \div \dfrac{8}{19}$

15) $\dfrac{3}{16} \div \dfrac{15}{32}$

16) $\dfrac{5}{7} \div \dfrac{1}{6}$

17) $\dfrac{16}{25} \div \dfrac{4}{5}$

18) $\dfrac{2}{17} \div \dfrac{2}{13}$

19) $9 \div \dfrac{1}{6}$

20) $\dfrac{12}{28} \div \dfrac{3}{7}$

21) $\dfrac{6}{17} \div \dfrac{5}{14}$

Adding and Subtracting Mixed Numbers

✎ **Add.**

1) $2\frac{1}{4} + 3\frac{1}{4}$

2) $5\frac{3}{4} + 2\frac{1}{4}$

3) $1\frac{1}{9} + 2\frac{2}{9}$

4) $3\frac{1}{6} + 2\frac{2}{3}$

5) $5\frac{4}{15} + 5\frac{3}{10}$

6) $4\frac{1}{7} + 1\frac{1}{3}$

7) $1\frac{5}{21} + 1\frac{5}{28}$

8) $3\frac{2}{5} + 1\frac{3}{7}$

9) $3\frac{3}{8} + 4\frac{1}{12}$

10) $12 + \frac{1}{8}$

11) $2\frac{5}{18} + \frac{5}{24}$

12) $4\frac{7}{16} + 1\frac{1}{2}$

✎ **Subtract.**

1) $4\frac{3}{8} - 1\frac{1}{8}$

2) $3\frac{7}{12} - \frac{1}{3}$

3) $5\frac{9}{14} - 5\frac{6}{21}$

4) $11\frac{4}{9} - 7\frac{1}{4}$

5) $3\frac{1}{3} - 2\frac{2}{3}$

6) $7\frac{1}{8} - 2\frac{1}{2}$

7) $5\frac{4}{17} - 2\frac{4}{17}$

8) $4\frac{10}{11} - 2\frac{1}{3}$

9) $4\frac{2}{7} - 3\frac{2}{5}$

10) $4\frac{5}{9} - 2\frac{7}{18}$

11) $5\frac{7}{15} - 3\frac{2}{15}$

12) $6\frac{1}{21} - 2\frac{1}{35}$

Multiplying and Dividing Mixed Numbers

✎ **Find each product.**

1) $1\frac{1}{4} \times 1\frac{1}{4}$

2) $2\frac{3}{7} \times 1\frac{2}{3}$

3) $4\frac{3}{5} \times 3\frac{3}{4}$

4) $4\frac{1}{8} \times 1\frac{2}{5}$

5) $3\frac{2}{3} \times 2\frac{1}{5}$

6) $1\frac{1}{9} \times 1\frac{2}{3}$

7) $4\frac{1}{2} \times 1\frac{3}{8}$

8) $4\frac{1}{2} \times 2\frac{1}{5}$

9) $2\frac{2}{3} \times 3\frac{1}{4}$

10) $3\frac{1}{5} \times 3\frac{3}{4}$

11) $1\frac{1}{6} \times 1\frac{1}{3}$

12) $1\frac{5}{9} \times 1\frac{4}{5}$

✎ **Find each quotient.**

1) $2\frac{3}{5} \div 1\frac{3}{5}$

2) $4\frac{1}{6} \div 1\frac{2}{3}$

3) $3\frac{2}{5} \div 1\frac{2}{15}$

4) $3\frac{3}{4} \div 2\frac{5}{8}$

5) $1\frac{3}{7} \div 1\frac{1}{2}$

6) $2\frac{5}{6} \div 2\frac{2}{3}$

7) $2\frac{2}{3} \div 3\frac{1}{5}$

8) $3\frac{1}{5} \div 2\frac{2}{3}$

9) $2\frac{1}{7} \div 1\frac{3}{5}$

10) $2\frac{7}{12} \div 6\frac{1}{5}$

11) $3\frac{2}{7} \div 1\frac{5}{9}$

12) $0 \div 1\frac{1}{2}$

Comparing Decimals

✍ Write the correct comparison symbol (>, < or =).

1) 1.15 _____ 2.15

2) 0.4 _____ 0.385

3) 12.5 _____ 12.500

4) 4.05 _____ 4.50

5) 0.511 _____ 0.51

6) 0.623 _____ 0.723

7) 8.76 _____ 8.678

8) 3.0069 _____ 3.069

9) 22.042 _____ 22.034

10) 5.11 _____ 5.08

11) 1.11 _____ 1.111

12) 0.06 _____ 0.55

13) 3.204 _____ 3.25

14) 3.92 _____ 3.0952

15) 0.44 _____ 0.044

16) 17.04 _____ 17.040

17) 0.090 _____ 0.80

18) 0.021 _____ 0.201

19) 0.0067 _____ 0.00089

20) 0.79 _____ 0.6

Rounding Decimals

✎ Round each decimal number to the nearest place indicated.

1) 0.6̲3

2) 3.0̲4

3) 7.6̲23

4) 0.3̲66

5) 7̲.707

6) 0.08̲8

7) 6.2̲4

8) 76.76̲0

9) 3.62̲9

10) 12.3̲858

11) 1.0̲9

12) 4.2̲57

13) 3.2̲43

14) 6.05̲40

15) 93̲.69

16) 37̲.45

17) 41̲7.078

18) 312.6̲55

19) 18.40̲09

20) 85̲.85

21) 3.20̲8

22) 57.0̲73

23) 126.5̲18

24) 7.00̲69

25) 0.01̲11

26) 11.340̲6

27) 6.3̲891

Adding and Subtracting Decimals

✎ **Add and subtract decimals.**

1)
$$\begin{array}{r} 37.69 \\ -\ 15.58 \\ \hline \end{array}$$

4)
$$\begin{array}{r} 84.10 \\ -\ 43.45 \\ \hline \end{array}$$

2)
$$\begin{array}{r} 56.93 \\ +\ 23.07 \\ \hline \end{array}$$

5)
$$\begin{array}{r} 121.26 \\ +\ 78.97 \\ \hline \end{array}$$

3)
$$\begin{array}{r} 18.96 \\ +\ 12.87 \\ \hline \end{array}$$

6)
$$\begin{array}{r} 65.00 \\ -\ 53.39 \\ \hline \end{array}$$

✎ **Solve.**

7) ___ $+\ 3.3 = 5.08$

10) $6.9 -$ ___ $= 0.047$

8) $5.05 +$ ___ $= 14.6$

11) ___ $+\ 0.074 = 1.084$

9) $12.9 -$ ___ $= 7.25$

12) ___ $-\ 6.62 = 31.72$

Multiplying and Dividing Decimals

✎ Find each product

$$\begin{array}{r} 5.5 \\ \times\ 2.6 \\ \hline \end{array}$$
1)

$$\begin{array}{r} 21.09 \\ \times\ 9.07 \\ \hline \end{array}$$
4)

$$\begin{array}{r} 6.9 \\ \times\ 0.8 \\ \hline \end{array}$$
7)

$$\begin{array}{r} 8.7 \\ \times\ 6.9 \\ \hline \end{array}$$
2)

$$\begin{array}{r} 14.3 \\ \times\ 15.7 \\ \hline \end{array}$$
5)

$$\begin{array}{r} 67.08 \\ \times\ 10 \\ \hline \end{array}$$
8)

$$\begin{array}{r} 4.06 \\ \times\ 7.05 \\ \hline \end{array}$$
3)

$$\begin{array}{r} 7.09 \\ \times\ 4.0 \\ \hline \end{array}$$
6)

$$\begin{array}{r} 12.08 \\ \times\ 1000 \\ \hline \end{array}$$
9)

✎ Find each quotient.

10) $18.7 \div 2.5$

13) $8.05 \div 2.5$

16) $7.38 \div 1000$

11) $45.2 \div 5$

14) $7.6 \div 100$

17) $36.1 \div 100$

12) $15.6 \div 4.5$

15) $2.07 \div 10$

18) $0.03 \div 10$

Converting Between Fractions, Decimals and Mixed Numbers

✎ Convert fractions to decimals

1) $\dfrac{5}{10}$

2) $\dfrac{36}{100}$

3) $\dfrac{5}{8}$

4) $\dfrac{15}{16}$

5) $\dfrac{6}{18}$

6) $\dfrac{40}{100}$

7) $\dfrac{32}{40}$

8) $\dfrac{14}{25}$

9) $\dfrac{73}{10}$

✎ Convert decimal into fraction or mixed numbers.

10) 0.7

11) 7.25

12) 0.44

13) 5.3

14) 0.16

15) 0.05

16) 0.18

17) 0.4

18) 0.06

19) 0.68

20) 4.6

21) 3.2

Answers of Worksheets – Chapter 2

Simplifying Fractions

1) $\frac{21}{31}$

2) $\frac{3}{4}$

3) $\frac{2}{3}$

4) $\frac{3}{4}$

5) $\frac{1}{3}$

6) $\frac{1}{4}$

7) $\frac{4}{9}$

8) $\frac{1}{2}$

9) $\frac{2}{5}$

10) $\frac{1}{9}$

11) $\frac{5}{9}$

12) $\frac{3}{4}$

13) $5\frac{5}{8}$

14) $2\frac{13}{16}$

15) $9\frac{1}{5}$

16) $3\frac{5}{8}$

17) $1\frac{1}{2}$

18) $4\frac{1}{5}$

19) $1\frac{3}{4}$

20) $\frac{9}{10}$

21) $7\frac{1}{2}$

Factoring Numbers

1) $1, 2, 4, 8, 16, 32$

2) $1, 2, 13, 26$

3) $1, 2, 4, 5, 8, 10, 20, 40$

4) $1, 2, 3, 4, 6, 8, 12\ 7, 16, 24, 32, 48, 96$

5) $1, 2, 3, 4, 5, 6, 10, 12, 15, 20, 30, 60$

6) $1, 2, 4, 7, 14, 28$

7) $1, 5, 7, 35$

8) $1, 2, 4, 8, 16, 32, 64$

9) $1, 2, 4, 7, 8, 14, 56$

10) $1, 3, 5, 15, 25, 75$

11) $1, 3, 9, 27, 81$

12) $1, 2, 3, 4, 6, 8, 12, 16, 24, 48$

13) $2 \times 2 \times 5$

14) 5×13

15) $3 \times 3 \times 11$

16) $3 \times 2 \times 7$

17) $2 \times 2 \times 3 \times 7$

18) $3 \times 2 \times 5$

19) $2 \times 2 \times 13$

20) $3 \times 5 \times 7$

21) $3 \times 5 \times 5$

22) $2 \times 2 \times 2 \times 2 \times 3$

23) $2 \times 2 \times 3 \times 3$

24) 31×1

25) $2 \times 2 \times 2 \times 3$

26) $2 \times 3 \times 3 \times 3$

Greatest Common Factor

1) 7	7) 4	13) 6
2) 1	8) 15	14) 15
3) 12	9) 36	15) 21
4) 5	10) 9	16) 25
5) 13	11) 16	17) 2
6) 19	12) 5	18) 31

Least Common Multiple

1) 18	7) 126	13) 96
2) 175	8) 84	14) 525
3) 192	9) 704	15) 168
4) 36	10) 60	16) 315
5) 42	11) 150	17) 336
6) 45	12) 40	18) 360

Divisibility Rules

1) 24   **2** **3** **4** 5 **6** 7 **8** 9 10

2) 32   **2** 3 **4** 5 6 7 **8** 9 10

3) 16   **2** 3 **4** 5 6 7 **8** 9 10

4) 42   **2** **3** 4 5 **6** **7** 8 9 10

5) 28   **2** 3 **4** 5 6 **7** 8 9 10

6) 56   **2** 3 **4** 5 6 **7** **8** 9 10

7) 48   **2** 3 **4** 5 **6** 7 **8** 9 10

8) 36   **2** **3** **4** 5 **6** 7 8 **9** 10

9) 81   2 **3** 4 5 6 7 8 **9** 10

10) 50   **2** 3 4 **5** 6 7 8 9 **10**

11) 63   2 **3** 4 5 6 **7** 8 **9** 10

12) 84   **2** 3 **4** 5 **6** 7 8 9 10

Adding and Subtracting Fractions

1) $\frac{5}{6}$

2) $\frac{20}{21}$

3) $\frac{55}{63}$

4) $\frac{3}{4}$

5) $\frac{7}{10}$

6) $\frac{3}{5}$

7) 1

8) $\frac{23}{26}$

9) $\frac{53}{112}$

10) $\frac{1}{2}$

11) $\frac{9}{40}$

12) $\frac{23}{42}$

13) $\frac{1}{72}$

14) $\frac{11}{60}$

15) $\frac{5}{16}$

16) $\frac{1}{75}$

17) $\frac{1}{36}$

18) $\frac{5}{112}$

Multiplying and Dividing Fractions

1) $\frac{3}{28}$

2) $\frac{1}{10}$

3) $\frac{1}{12}$

4) $\frac{4}{11}$

5) $\frac{3}{5}$

6) $\frac{36}{85}$

7) 0

8) 1

9) $\frac{1}{6}$

10) 0

11) $\frac{1}{12}$

12) $\frac{8}{11}$

13) $\frac{3}{4}$

14) $\frac{1}{2}$

15) $\frac{2}{5}$

16) $\frac{30}{7}$

17) $\frac{4}{5}$

18) $\frac{13}{17}$

19) 54

20) 1

21) $\frac{84}{85}$

Adding Mixed Numbers

1) $5\frac{1}{2}$

2) 8

3) $3\frac{1}{3}$

4) $5\frac{5}{6}$

5) $10\frac{17}{30}$

6) $5\frac{10}{21}$

7) $2\frac{5}{12}$

8) $4\frac{29}{35}$

9) $7\frac{11}{24}$

10) $12\frac{1}{8}$

11) $2\frac{35}{72}$

12) $5\frac{15}{16}$

Subtract Mixed Numbers

1) $3\frac{1}{4}$

2) $3\frac{1}{4}$

3) $\frac{5}{14}$

4) $4\frac{7}{36}$

5) $\frac{2}{3}$

6) $4\frac{5}{8}$

7) 3

8) $2\frac{19}{33}$

9) $\frac{31}{35}$

10) $2\frac{1}{6}$

11) $2\frac{1}{3}$

12) $4\frac{2}{35}$

Multiplying Mixed Numbers

1) $1\frac{9}{16}$

2) $4\frac{1}{21}$

3) $5\frac{10}{21}$

4) $5\frac{31}{40}$

5) $8\frac{1}{15}$

6) $1\frac{23}{27}$

7) $6\frac{3}{16}$

8) $9\frac{9}{10}$

9) $8\frac{2}{3}$

10) 12

11) $1\frac{5}{9}$

12) $2\frac{4}{5}$

Dividing Mixed Numbers

1) $1\frac{5}{8}$

2) $2\frac{1}{2}$

3) 3

4) $1\frac{3}{7}$

5) $\frac{20}{21}$

6) $1\frac{1}{16}$

7) $\frac{5}{6}$

8) $1\frac{1}{5}$

9) $1\frac{19}{56}$

10) $\frac{5}{12}$

11) $2\frac{11}{98}$

12) 0

Comparing Decimals

1) <

2) >

3) =

4) <

5) >

6) <

7) >

8) <

9) >

10) >

11) <

12) <

13) <

14) >

15) >

16) =

17) <

18) <

19) >

20) >

Rounding Decimals

1) 1.0

2) 3.0

3) 7.6

4) 0.4

5) 8

6) 0.09

7) 6.2

8) 76.76

9) 3.63

10) 12.4

11) 1.1

12) 4.3

13) 3.2

14) 6.05

15) 94

16) 37

17) 420

18) 312.7

19) 18.4

20) 86

21) 3.21

22) 57.1

23) 126.5

24) 7.01

25) 0.01

26) 11.34

27) 6.4

Adding and Subtracting Decimals

1) 22.11

2) 80

3) 31.83

4) 40.65

5) 200.23

6) 11.61

7) 1.78

8) 9.55

9) 5.65

10) 6.853

11) 1.01

12) 38.34

Multiplying and Dividing Decimals

1) 14.3

2) 60.03

3) 28.623

4) 191.2863

5) 224.51

6) 28.36

7) 5.52

8) 670.8

9) 12080

10) 7.48

11) 9.04

12) 3.46...

13) 3.22

14) 0.207

15) 0.076

16) 0.00738

17) 0.361

18) 0.003

Converting Between Fractions, Decimals and Mixed Numbers

1) 0.5

2) 0.36

3) 0.625

4) 0.9375

5) 0.333...

6) 0.4

7) 0.8

8) 0.56

9) 7.3

10) $\frac{7}{10}$

11) $7\frac{1}{4}$

12) $\frac{11}{25}$

13) $5\frac{3}{10}$

14) $\frac{4}{25}$

15) $\frac{1}{20}$

16) $\frac{9}{50}$

17) $\frac{2}{5}$

18) $\frac{3}{50}$

19) $\frac{17}{25}$

20) $4\frac{3}{5}$

21) $3\frac{1}{5}$

Chapter 3: Proportion, Ratio, Percent

Topics that you'll learn in this chapter:

- ✓ Writing and Simplifying Ratios

- ✓ Create a Proportion

- ✓ Similar Figures

- ✓ Simple Interest

- ✓ Ratio and Rates Word Problems

- ✓ Percentage Calculations

- ✓ Converting Between Percent, Fractions, and Decimals

- ✓ Percent Problems

- ✓ Markup, Discount, and Tax

"Do not worry about your difficulties in mathematics. I can assure you mine are still greater." – Albert Einstein

Writing and Simplifying Ratios

📝 **Express each ratio as a rate and unite rate.**

1) 75 dollars for 5 chairs.

2) 203miles on 7 gallons of gas.

3) 168 miles on 3 hours

4) 16 inches of snow in 24 hours

5) 42 dimes t0 126 dimes

6) 27 feet out of 81 feet

📝 **Express each ratio as a fraction in the simplest form.**

7) 17 cups to 51 cups

8) 24 cakes out of 60 cakes

9) 42 red desks out of 189 desks

10) 45 story books out of 72 books

11) 28 gallons to 40 gallons

12) 68 miles out of 100 miles

📝 **Reduce each ratio.**

1) 24: 42

2) 45: 15

3) 28: 36

4) 24: 26

5) 14: 56

6) 48: 60

7) 108: 252

8) 81: 45

9) 100: 25

10) 18: 32

11) 60: 10

12) 35: 45

13) 76: 57

14) 10: 100

15) 16: 40

16) 17: 34

17) 5: 25

18) 66: 39

Create a Proportion

✎ Create proportion from the given set of numbers

1) 2, 1, 8, 4

4) 11, 15, 22, 30

7) 32, 2, 16, 4

2) 7, 24, 56, 3

5) 5, 30, 75, 2

8) 63, 12, 9, 84

3) 21, 18, 63, 6

6) 9, 7, 54, 42

9) 10, 10, 100, 1

Similar Figures

✎ Each pair of figures is similar. Find the missing side.

1)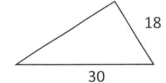

2)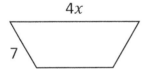

3)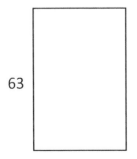

Ratio and Rates Word Problems

Solve.

1) In Peter's class, 27 of the students are tall and 15 are short. In Elise's class 81 students are tall and 45 students are short. Which class has a higher ratio of tall to short students?

2) In a party, 12 soft drinks are required for every 26 guests. If there are 364 guests, how many soft drinks is required?

3) The price of 6 bananas at the first Market is $1.08. The price of 4 of the same bananas at second Market is $0.76. Which place is the better buy?

4) You can buy 4 cans of green beans at a supermarket for $2.40. How much does it cost to buy 32 cans of green beans?

5) The bakers at a Bakery can make 132 bagels in 6 hours. How many bagels can they bake in 8 hours? What is that rate per hour?

Percentage Calculations

✒ **Calculate the percentages.**

1) 25% of 38

2) 42% of 8

3) 15% of 15

4) 63% of 75

5) 4% of 50

6) 35% of 14

7) 18% of 3

8) 9% of 47

9) 10% of 100

10) 50% of 72

11) 75% of 60

12) 95% of 12

13) 80% of 30

14) 11% of 120

15) 1% of 210

16) 32% of 0

✒ **Solve.**

17) What percentage of 40 is 2

18) 13.2 is what percentage of 88?

19) 38 is what percentage of 76?

20) Find what percentage of 85 is 22.1.

Percent Problems

✍ **Solve each problem.**

1) 64% of what number is 16?

2) What is 70% of 140 inches?

3) What percent of 58 is 23.2?

4) 8 is 250% of what?

5) 18 is what percent of 20?

6) 34 is 40% of what?

7) 9 is what percent of 12?

8) 95% of 100 is what number?

9) Mia require 60% to pass. If she gets 240 marks and falls short by 60 marks, what were the maximum marks she could have got?

10) Jack scored 34 out of 40 marks in mathematics, 8 out of 10 marks in history and 78 out of 100 marks in science. In which subject his percentage of marks is the best?

Markup, Discount, and Tax

✍ **Find the selling price of each item.**

1) Cost of a chair: $18.99, markup: 25%, discount: 8%, tax: 8%

2) Cost of computer: $1,490.00, markup: 60%

3) Cost of a pen: $2.50, markup: 60%, discount: 20%, tax: 5%

4) Cost of a puppy: $1,900, markup: 38%, discount: 15%

Simple Interest

✎ **Use simple interest to find the ending balance.**

1) $3,200 at 13.7% for 2 years.

2) $280,000 at 3.75% for 15 years.

3) $2,000 at 1.9% for 5 years.

4) $14,700 at 5.8% for 3 years.

5) $47,500 at 0.5% for 16 months.

6) Emily puts $4,500 into an investment yielding 2.75% annual simple interest; she left the money in for six years. How much interest does Sara get at the end of those six years?

7) A new car, valued at $36,000, depreciates at 8.5% per year from original price. Find the value of the car 5 years after purchase.

8) $360 interest is earned on a principal of $1,800 at a simple interest rate of 5% interest per year. For how many years was the principal invested?

Converting Between Percent, Fractions, and Decimals

Converting fractions to decimals

1) $\frac{40}{100}$ 4) $\frac{1}{10}$ 7) $\frac{40}{50}$

2) $\frac{28}{100}$ 5) $\frac{7}{20}$ 8) $\frac{25}{10}$

3) $\frac{4}{25}$ 6) $\frac{2}{100}$ 9) $\frac{6}{30}$

Write each decimal as a percent.

10) 0.25   15) 0.2

11) 1.2   16) 1.05

12) 0.015   17) 0.0275

13) 0.005   18) 0.0025

14) 0.725   19) 0.175

Answers of Worksheets – Chapter 3

Writing Ratios

1) $\frac{75\ dollars}{5\ books}$, 15.00 dollars per chair

2) $\frac{203\ miles}{7\ gallons}$, 29 miles per gallon

3) $\frac{168\ miles}{3\ hours}$, 56 miles per hour

4) $\frac{120"\ of\ snow}{24\ hours}$, 5 inches of snow per hour

5) $\frac{126\ dimes}{42\ dimes}$, 3 per dime

6) $\frac{108\ feet}{27\ feet}$, 4 per foot

7) $\frac{1}{3}$

8) $\frac{2}{5}$

9) $\frac{2}{9}$

10) $\frac{5}{8}$

11) $\frac{7}{10}$

12) $\frac{17}{25}$

Reduce each Ratio

1) 4: 7

2) 3: 1

3) 7: 9

4) 12: 13

5) 1: 4

6) 4: 5

7) 3: 7

8) 9: 5

9) 4: 1

10) 9: 16

11) 6: 1

12) 7: 9

13) 4: 3

14) 1: 10

15) 2: 5

16) 1: 2

17) 1: 5

18) 22: 13

Create a Proportion

1) 1: 4 = 2: 8

2) 3: 24 = 7: 56

3) 6: 18 = 21: 63

4) 11: 22 = 15: 30

5) 5: 75=2: 30

6) 7: 42 =9: 54

7) 2: 16 =4: 32

8) 9: 63 =12: 84

9) 1: 10 =10: 100

Similar Figures

1) 5

2) 2

3) 2

Ratio and Rates Word Problems

1) The ratio for both classes is equal to 9 to 5.

2) 168

3) The price at the first Market is a better buy.

4) $19.20

5) 176, the rate is 22 per hour.

Percentage Calculations

1) 9.5	6) 4.9	11) 45	16) 0
2) 3.36	7) 0.54	12) 11.4	17) 5%
3) 2.25	8) 4.23	13) 24	18) 15%
4) 47.25	9) 10	14) 13.2	19) 50%
5) 2	10) 36	15) 2.1	20) 26%

Percent Problems

1) 25	5) 90%	9) 500
2) 98	6) 85	10) Mathematics
3) 40%	7) 75%	
4) 3.2	8) 95	

Markup, Discount, and Tax

1) $23.59	3) $3.36
2) $2,384	4) $2,228.70

Simple Interest

1) $4,076.80	4) $17,257.80	7) $20,700
2) $437,500.00	5) $51,300.00	8) 4 years
3) $2,190.00	6) $742.50	

Converting Between Percent, Fractions, and Decimals

1) 0.4	4) 0.1	7) 0.8
2) 0.28	5) 0.35	8) 2.5
3) 0.16	6) 0.02	9) 0.2

10) 25%

11) 120%

12) 1.5%

13) 0.5%

14) 72.5%

15) 20%

16) 105%

17) 2.75%

18) 0.25%

19) 17.5%

Chapter 4: Exponents and Radicals

Topics that you'll learn in this chapter:

✓ Multiplication Property of Exponents

✓ Division Property of Exponents

✓ Powers of Products and Quotients

✓ Zero, Negative Exponents and Bases

Mathematics is no more computation than typing is literature.

– John Allen Paulos

Multiplication Property of Exponents

✎ Simplify.

1) $3^2 \times 3^2$

2) $4 . 4^2 . 4^2$

3) $2^2 . 2^2$

4) $5x^3 . x$

5) $14x^4 . 2x$

6) $5x . 2x^2$

7) $6x^4 . 7x^4$

8) $4x^2 . 6x^3 y^4$

9) $8x^2 y^5 . 8xy^3$

10) $5xy^4 . 4x^3 y^3$

11) $(3x^2)^2$

12) $4x^5 y^3 . 5x^2 y^3$

13) $7x^3 . 10y^3 x^5 . 7yx^3$

14) $(x^4)^3$

15) $(3x^2)^4$

16) $8x^4 y^5 . 2x^2 y^3$

Division Property of Exponents

✎ Simplify.

1) $\dfrac{5^6}{5}$

2) $\dfrac{43}{43^{45}}$

3) $\dfrac{3^2}{3^3}$

4) $\dfrac{5^4}{5^2}$

5) $\dfrac{x}{x^{13}}$

6) $\dfrac{24x^3}{6x^4}$

7) $\dfrac{2x^{-5}}{11x^{-2}}$

8) $\dfrac{49x^8}{7x^3}$

9) $\dfrac{11x^6}{4x^7}$

10) $\dfrac{42x^2}{4x^3}$

14) $\dfrac{12x^3}{6y^8}$

18) $\dfrac{12x^4}{15x^7y^9}$

11) $\dfrac{x}{10x^3}$

15) $\dfrac{25xy^4}{x^6y^2}$

19) $\dfrac{yx^4}{10yx^8}$

12) $\dfrac{x^3}{2x^5}$

16) $\dfrac{2x^4}{7x}$

20) $\dfrac{16x^4y}{9x^8y^2}$

13) $\dfrac{16x^3}{14x^6}$

17) $\dfrac{32x^2y^8}{4x^3}$

21) $\dfrac{6x^8}{36x^8}$

Powers of Products and Quotients

✎ Simplify.

1) $(x^3)^4$

8) $(5x^4y^3)^4$

15) $(10x^{11}y^3)^2$

2) $(2xy^4)^2$

9) $(4x^6y^8)^2$

16) $(8x^7\,y^5)^2$

3) $(6x^4)^2$

10) $(15x^3.x)^3$

17) $(9x^4y^6)^5$

4) $(12x^5)^2$

11) $(x^9\,x^6)^3$

18) $(3x^4)^2$

5) $(2x^2y^4)^4$

12) $(7x^{10}y^3)^3$

19) $(3x\,4y^3)^2$

6) $(3x^4y^4)^3$

13) $(6x^3\,x^2)^2$

20) $(7x^2y)^3$

7) $(4x^2y^2)^2$

14) $(4x^3\,5x)^2$

21) $(14x^2y^5)^2$

Zero and Negative Exponents

✎ Evaluate the following expressions.

1) 5^{-2}

2) 3^4

3) 7^{-2}

4) 5^{-4}

5) 12^{-1}

6) 7^{-1}

7) 6^{-2}

8) 8^{-2}

9) 5^{-2}

10) 15^{-1}

11) 7^{-3}

12) 0^5

13) 10^{-7}

14) 4^{-4}

15) 4^{-2}

16) 2^{-3}

17) 3^{-4}

18) 6^{-1}

19) 7^3

20) 11^{-2}

21) $\left(\frac{3}{4}\right)^{-2}$

22) $\left(\frac{1}{5}\right)^{-2}$

23) $\left(\frac{1}{2}\right)^{-6}$

24) $\left(\frac{2}{5}\right)^{-2}$

25) 10^{-4}

26) 1^{-100}

Negative Exponents and Negative Bases

✎ Simplify.

1) -4^{-1}

2) $-5x^{-3}$

3) $\frac{x}{x^{-3}}$

4) $-\frac{a^{-6}}{b^{-2}}$

5) $\frac{5}{x^{-3}}$

6) $\frac{b}{-9c^{-4}}$

7) $-\frac{25n^{-2}}{10p^{-3}}$

8) $\frac{4ab^{-2}}{-3c^{-2}}$

9) $10x^2y^{-3}$

10) $\left(-\frac{1}{4}\right)^{-2}$

11) $\left(-\frac{5}{4}\right)^{-2}$

12) $\left(\frac{x}{3yz}\right)^{-3}$

Writing Scientific Notation

✎ Write each number in scientific notation.

1) 81×10^5

2) 50

3) 0.0000008

4) 254000

5) 0.000225

6) 6.5

7) 0.00063

8) 89000000

9) 9000000

10) 85000000

11) 0.0000036

12) 0.00015

13) 0.008

14) 8600

15) 1960

16) 170000

17) 0.115

18) 0.05

Square Roots

✎ Find the value each square root.

1) $\sqrt{81}$

2) $\sqrt{0}$

3) $\sqrt{36}$

4) $\sqrt{64}$

5) $\sqrt{49}$

6) $\sqrt{1}$

7) $\sqrt{25}$

8) $\sqrt{9}$

9) $\sqrt{144}$

10) $\sqrt{121}$

11) $\sqrt{16}$

12) $\sqrt{256}$

13) $\sqrt{100}$

14) $\sqrt{169}$

15) $\sqrt{324}$

16) $\sqrt{90}$

17) $\sqrt{484}$

18) $\sqrt{529}$

Simplifying Radical Expressions

✎ *Simplify.*

1) $\sqrt{33x^2}$

2) $\sqrt{40x^2}$

3) $\sqrt{25x^3}$

4) $\sqrt{144a}$

5) $\sqrt{512v}$

6) $\sqrt{9x^2}$

7) $\sqrt{384}$

8) $\sqrt{162p^3}$

9) $\sqrt{125m^4}$

10) $\sqrt{693x^3y^3}$

11) $\sqrt{81x^3y^3}$

12) $\sqrt{9a^4b^3}$

13) $\sqrt{40x^3y^3}$

14) $3\sqrt{45x^2}$

15) $5\sqrt{60x^2}$

16) $4\sqrt{81a}$

17) $3\sqrt{8x^2y^3r}$

18) $4\sqrt{64x^2y^3z^4}$

Simplifying Radical Expressions Involving Fractions

✍ *Simplify.*

1) $\dfrac{2\sqrt{7r}}{\sqrt{m^4}}$

2) $\dfrac{6\sqrt{2}}{\sqrt{k}}$

3) $\dfrac{\sqrt{c}}{\sqrt{c}+\sqrt{d}}$

4) $\dfrac{5+\sqrt{3}}{2-\sqrt{3}}$

5) $\dfrac{2+\sqrt{7}}{6-\sqrt{5}}$

6) $\dfrac{3}{2+\sqrt{3}}$

7) $\dfrac{\sqrt{6}-\sqrt{4}}{\sqrt{4}-\sqrt{6}}$

8) $\dfrac{\sqrt{3}}{\sqrt{7}-2}$

9) $\dfrac{\sqrt{2}-\sqrt{6}}{\sqrt{2}+\sqrt{6}}$

10) $\dfrac{3\sqrt{5}+5}{2\sqrt{5}-3}$

11) $\dfrac{\sqrt{8a^5b^3}}{\sqrt{2ab^2}}$

12) $\dfrac{6\sqrt{20x^3}}{3\sqrt{5x}}$

Multiplying Radical Expressions

✎ Simplify.

1) $\sqrt{12x} \times \sqrt{12x}$

10) $-3\sqrt{8}\,(2 + \sqrt{8})$

2) $-5\sqrt{27} \times -3\sqrt{3}$

11) $\sqrt{12x}\,(3 - \sqrt{6x})$

3) $3\sqrt{45x^2} \times \sqrt{5x^2}$

12) $\sqrt{3x}\,(x^3 + \sqrt{27})$

4) $\sqrt{8x^2} \times \sqrt{12x^3}$

13) $\sqrt{15r}\,(2 + \sqrt{3})$

5) $-10\sqrt{8} \times \sqrt{5x^3}$

14) $\sqrt{2v}\,(\sqrt{6} + \sqrt{10})$

6) $5\sqrt{21} \times \sqrt{3}$

15) $(-2\sqrt{6} + 3)\,(\sqrt{6} - 1)$

7) $\sqrt{3} \times -\sqrt{64}$

16) $(2 - \sqrt{3})(-2 + \sqrt{3})$

8) $-5\sqrt{16x^3} \times 4\sqrt{2x^2}$

17) $(10 - 4\sqrt{5})(6 - \sqrt{5})$

9) $\sqrt{12}\,(2 + \sqrt{3})$

18) $(\sqrt{6} - \sqrt{3})(\sqrt{6} + \sqrt{3})$

Adding and Subtracting Radical Expressions

✎ *Simplify.*

1) $6\sqrt{10} + 4\sqrt{10}$

2) $-3\sqrt{12} - 3\sqrt{27}$

3) $-3\sqrt{22} - 5\sqrt{22}$

4) $-9\sqrt{7} + 12\sqrt{7}$

5) $6\sqrt{3} - \sqrt{27}$

6) $-\sqrt{18} + 4\sqrt{2}$

7) $-4\sqrt{7} + 4\sqrt{7}$

8) $3\sqrt{27} + 3\sqrt{3}$

9) $2\sqrt{20} - 2\sqrt{5}$

10) $3\sqrt{18} - \sqrt{2}$

11) $-10\sqrt{35} + 14\sqrt{35}$

12) $-4\sqrt{19} - 5\sqrt{19}$

13) $-3\sqrt{6x} - 3\sqrt{6x}$

14) $\sqrt{5y^2} + y\sqrt{20}$

15) $\sqrt{8mn^2} + n\sqrt{18m}$

16) $-8\sqrt{27a} - 2\sqrt{3a}$

17) $-6\sqrt{7ab} - 6\sqrt{7ab}$

18) $\sqrt{27a^2b} + a\sqrt{12b}$

Solving Radical Equations

✍ *Solve each equation. Remember to check for extraneous solutions.*

1) $\sqrt{x-6} = 3$

2) $2 = \sqrt{x-3}$

3) $\sqrt{r} = 5$

4) $\sqrt{m+8} = 4$

5) $5\sqrt{3x} = 15$

6) $1 = \sqrt{x-4}$

7) $-18 = -6\sqrt{r+3}$

8) $10 = 2\sqrt{35v}$

9) $\sqrt{n+3} - 1 = 6$

10) $\sqrt{3r} = \sqrt{2r-2}$

11) $\sqrt{3x+15} = \sqrt{x+5}$

12) $\sqrt{v} = \sqrt{2v-5}$

13) $\sqrt{12-x} = \sqrt{x-2}$

14) $\sqrt{m+5} = \sqrt{3m+5}$

15) $\sqrt{2r+20} = \sqrt{-16-2r}$

16) $\sqrt{k+5} = \sqrt{1-k}$

17) $-10\sqrt{x-10} = -50$

18) $\sqrt{36-x} = \sqrt{\dfrac{x}{5}}$

Domain and Range of Radical Functions

✎Identify the domain and range of each.

1) $y = \sqrt{x + 4} - 3$

2) $y = \sqrt[3]{x - 3} + 6$

3) $y = \sqrt{x - 2} - 2$

4) $y = \sqrt[3]{x + 1} - 5$

Sketch the graph of each function.

5) $y = \sqrt{x} + 2$

6) $y = 3\sqrt{-x} - 2$

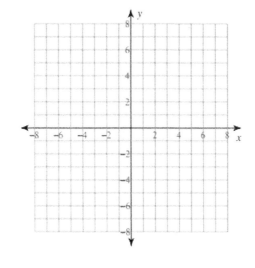
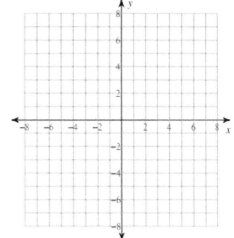

Answers of Worksheets – Chapter 4

Multiplication Property of Exponents

1) 3^4

2) 4^5

3) 2^4

4) $5x^4$

5) $48x^5$

6) $10x^3$

7) $42x^8$

8) $24x^5y^4$

9) $64x^3y^8$

10) $20x^4y^7$

11) $9x^4$

12) $20x^7y^6$

13) $490x^{11}y^4$

14) x^{12}

15) $81x^8$

16) $16x^6y^8$

Division Property of Exponents

1) 5^5

2) $\frac{1}{43^{44}}$

3) $\frac{1}{3}$

4) 5^2

5) $\frac{1}{x^{12}}$

6) $\frac{4}{x}$

7) $\frac{2}{11x^3}$

8) $7x^5$

9) $\frac{11}{4x}$

10) $\frac{21}{2x}$

11) $\frac{1}{10x^2}$

12) $\frac{1}{2x^2}$

13) $\frac{8}{7x^3}$

14) $\frac{2x^3}{y^8}$

15) $\frac{25y^2}{x^5}$

16) $\frac{2x^3}{7}$

17) $\frac{8y^8}{x}$

18) $\frac{4}{5x^3y^9}$

19) $\frac{1}{10x^4}$

20) $\frac{16}{9x^4y}$

21) $\frac{1}{6}$

Powers of Products and Quotients

1) x^{12}

2) $4x^2y^8$

3) $36x^8$

4) $124x^{10}$

5) $16x^8y^{16}$

6) $27x^{12}y^{12}$

7) $16x^4y^4$

8) $625x^{16}y^{12}$

9) $16x^{12}y^{16}$

10) $3,375x^{12}$

11) x^{45}

12) $343x^{30}y^9$

13) $36x^{10}$

14) $350x^8$

15) $100x^{22}y^6$

16) $64x^{14}y^{10}$

17) $59,049x^{20}y^{30}$

18) $9x^8$

19) $144x^2y^6$

20) $343x^6y^3$

21) $196x^4y^{10}$

Zero and Negative Exponents

1) $\frac{1}{25}$

2) 81

3) $\frac{1}{49}$

4) $\frac{1}{625}$

5) $\frac{1}{12}$

6) $\frac{1}{7}$

7) $\frac{1}{36}$

8) $\frac{1}{64}$

9) $\frac{1}{25}$

10) $\frac{1}{15}$

11) $\frac{1}{343}$

12) 0

13) $\frac{1}{10000000}$

14) $\frac{1}{256}$

15) $\frac{1}{16}$

16) $\frac{1}{8}$

17) $\frac{1}{81}$

18) $\frac{1}{6}$

19) 343

20) $\frac{1}{121}$

21) $\frac{16}{9}$

22) 25

23) 64

24) $\frac{25}{4}$

25) $\frac{1}{10000}$

26) 1

Negative Exponents and Negative Bases

1) $-\frac{1}{4}$

2) $-\frac{5}{x^3}$

3) x^4

4) $-\frac{b^2}{a^6}$

5) $5x^3$

6) $-\frac{bc^4}{9}$

7) $-\frac{5p^3}{2n^2}$

8) $-\frac{4ac^2}{3b^2}$

9) $\frac{10x^2}{y^3}$

10) 16

11) $\frac{16}{25}$

12) $\frac{27y^3z^3}{x^3}$

Writing Scientific Notation

1) 8.1×10^6

2) 5×10^1

3) 8×10^{-7}

4) 2.54×10^5

5) 2.25×10^{-4}

6) 6.5×10^0

7) 6.3×10^{-4}

8) 8.9×10^7

9) 9×10^6

10) 8.5×10^7

11) 3.6×10^{-6}

12) 1.5×10^{-4}

13) 8×10^{-3}

14) 8.6×10^3

15) 1.96×10^3

16) 1.7×10^5

17) 1.15×10^{-1}

18) 5×10^{-2}

Square Roots

1) 9

2) 0

3) 6

4) 8

5) 7

6) 1

7) 5

8) 3

9) 12

10) 11

11) 4

12) 16

13) 10

14) 13

15) 18

16) 30

17) 22   18) 23

Simplifying radical expressions

1) $\sqrt{33}\,x$

2) $2x\sqrt{10}$

3) $5x\,\sqrt{x}$

4) $12\,\sqrt{a}$

5) $8\,\sqrt{8v}$

6) $3x$

7) $8\,\sqrt{6}$

8) $9p\,\sqrt{2p}$

9) $5m^2\,\sqrt{5}$

10) $3x.\,y\,\sqrt{77xy}$

11) $9x.\,y\,\sqrt{xy}$

12) $3a^2.\,b\,\sqrt{b}$

13) $2x.\,y\,\sqrt{10xy}$

14) $9x\,\sqrt{5}$

15) $10x\,\sqrt{15}$

16) $36\,\sqrt{a}$

17) $6x\,y\,\sqrt{2yr}$

18) $32z^2.\,x.\,y\,\sqrt{y}$

Simplifying radical expressions involving fractions

1) $\frac{2\sqrt{7r}}{m^2}$

2) $\frac{6\sqrt{2k}}{k}$

3) $\frac{c-\sqrt{cd}}{c-d}$

4) $13+7\,\sqrt{3}$

5) $\frac{2\sqrt{7}+6\sqrt{5}}{31}$

6) $6 - 3\,\sqrt{3}$

7) -1

8) $\frac{\sqrt{21}+2\sqrt{3}}{3}$

9) $2+\sqrt{3}$

10) $\frac{19\sqrt{5}+45}{11}$

11) $2a^2\,\sqrt{b}$

12) $4x$

Multiplying radical expressions

1) $12x$

2) 135

3) $45x^2$

4) $4x^{2.}\,\sqrt{6x}$

5) $-20x^{2.}\,\sqrt{10}$

6) $15\sqrt{7}$

7) $-8\,\sqrt{3}$

8) $-80x^2\,\sqrt{2x}$

9) $4\,\sqrt{3}+6$

10) $-(12\,\sqrt{2}+24)$

11) $6\,\sqrt{3x}-6x\,\sqrt{2}$

12) $\sqrt{3}.\,x^2+9x$

13) $3\sqrt{5r}+2\sqrt{15r}$

14) $2\,\sqrt{3v}+2\sqrt{5v}$

15) $5\sqrt{6}-15$

16) $4\sqrt{3}-7$

17) $80-34\sqrt{5}$

18) 3

Adding and subtracting radical expressions

1) $10\sqrt{10}$

2) $-15\sqrt{3}$

3) $-8\sqrt{22}$

4) $3\sqrt{7}$

5) $3\sqrt{3}$

6) $\sqrt{2}$

7) 0

8) $12\sqrt{3}$

9) $2\sqrt{5}$

10) $8\sqrt{2}$

11) $4\sqrt{35}$

12) $-9\sqrt{19}$

13) $-6\sqrt{6x}$

14) $3y\sqrt{5}$

15) $5n\sqrt{2m}$

16) $-26\sqrt{3}\,a$

17) $-12\sqrt{7ab}$

18) $5a\sqrt{3b}$

Solving radical equations

1) $\{15\}$

2) $\{7\}$

3) $\{25\}$

4) $\{8\}$

5) $\{3\}$

6) $\{5\}$

7) $\{0\}$

8) $\{\frac{5}{7}\}$

9) $\{46\}$

10) $\{-2\}$

11) $\{-5\}$

12) $\{5\}$

13) $\{7\}$

14) $\{0\}$

15) $\{-9\}$

16) $\{-2\}$

17) $\{35\}$

18) $\{30\}$

Domain and range of radical functions

1) domain: $x \geq -4$

   range: $y \geq -3$

2) domain: {all real numbers}

   range: {all real numbers}

3) domain: $x \geq 3$

   range: $y \geq 6$

4) domain: {all real numbers}

   range: {all real numbers}

5)

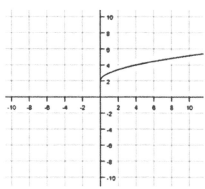

6)

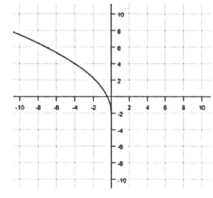

Chapter 5: Algebraic Expressions

Topics that you'll learn in this chapter:

- ✓ Expressions and Variables
- ✓ Simplifying Variable and Polynomial Expressions
- ✓ Translate Phrases into an Algebraic Statement
- ✓ The Distributive Property
- ✓ Evaluating One and two Variable
- ✓ Combining like Terms

Without mathematics, there's nothing you can do. Everything around you are mathematics. Everything around you are numbers." – Shakuntala Devi

Translate Phrases into an Algebraic Statement

✍ Write an algebraic expression for each phrase.

1) Ten subtracted from a number.

2) The quotient of fifteen and a number.

3) A number increased by forty.

4) A number divided by − 10.

5) The difference between fifty–two and a number.

6) Twice a number decreased by 35.

7) five times the sum of a number and − 12.

8) The quotient of 50 and the product of a number and − 6.

The Distributive Property

✍ Use the distributive property to simply each expression.

1) $6(8 - 2x)$

2) $-(-4 - 2x)$

3) $(-6x + 3)(-1)$

4) $(-4)(x - 2)$

5) $2(10 + 2x)$

6) $(-6x + 8)2$

7) $(3 - 6x)(-2)$

8) $(-12)(x + 1)$

9) $(-4)(x - 2) + 3(x + 1)$

10) $(-x)(-1 + 4x) - 4x(2 + 3x)$

11) $3(-5x - 1) + 4(2 - 3x)$

12) $(-2)(x + 2) - (4 + 3x)$

Evaluating One Variable

✍Simplify each algebraic expression.

1) $3x + 2, x = 2$

2) $x + (-4), x = -2$

3) $-2x - 5, x = -1$

4) $\left(-\frac{32}{x}\right) - 9 + x, x = 4$

5) $\frac{35}{x} - 3, x = 7$

6) $(-2) + \frac{x}{4} + 4x, x = 8$

7) $10 + 3x - 2, x = -2$

8) $(-2) + \frac{x}{7}, x = 49$

9) $\left(-\frac{18}{x}\right) - 9 + 2x, x = 2$

10) $(-2) + \frac{3x}{8}, x = 32$

Evaluating Two Variables

✍Simplify each algebraic expression.

1) $6a - (6 - b),$

$\qquad a = 3, b = 2$

2) $4x + 2y - 4 + 2,$

$\qquad x = 2, y = 3$

3) $\left(-\frac{18}{x}\right) + 1 + 5y,$

$\qquad x = 9, y = 2$

4) $(-2)(-2a - 2b),$

$\qquad a = 4, b = 2$

5) $6x + 2 - 2y,$

$\qquad x = 6, y = 8$

6) $8 + 2(-2x - 3y),$

$\qquad x = 1, y = 4$

7) $10x + y,$

$\qquad x = 6, y = 9$

8) $x \times 4 \div y,$

$\qquad x = 3, y = 2$

Expressions and Variables

✎ Simplify each expression.

1) $5(-2 - 9x), x = 2$

2) $-2(6 - 6x) - 3x, x = 1$

3) $x - 6x, x = 5$

4) $2x + 10x, x = 4$

5) $9 - 3x + 9x + 3, x = 1$

6) $5(3x + 2), x = 3$

7) $2(3 - 2x) - 6, x = 2$

8) $5x + 2x - 8, x = 2$

9) $3x + 6y, \ x = 5, y = 3$

10) $2x + 5x, x = 4,$

11) $5(-2x + 9) + 4, x = 7,$

12) $8x - 2x - 5, x = 2,$

13) $2x - 3x - 9, x = 5$

14) $(-4)(-2x - 8y), x = 3, y = 1$

15) $8x + 3 + 6y, x = 4, y = 3$

16) $(-6)(-8x - 9y), x = 3, y = 3$

Combining like Terms

✎ **Simplify each expression.**

1) $-6(-3x + 2)$

2) $3(-4 + 2x)$

3) $-4 - 4x + 6x + 9$

4) $6x - 3x - 5 + 8$

5) $(-3)(6x - 2) + 18$

6) $3(3x + 4) + 8x$

7) $2(-4x - 7) + 4(3x + 2)$

8) $(2x - 3y)3 + 5y$

9) $2.5x^2 \times (-6x)$

10) $-3 - x^2 - 8x^2$

11) $6 + 10x^2 + 2$

12) $9(-2x - 6) + 8$

13) $6x^2 + 4x + 5x^2$

14) $4x^2 - 10x^2 + 16x$

15) $4x^2 - 6x - x$

16) $(-4)(5x - 3)$

17) $3x + 6(2 - 2x)$

18) $10x + 3(18x - 4)$

19) $2(x + 8)$

20) $-3(x + 1) + 2x$

21) $x - 6y + 6x + 3y - 4x$

22) $7(-2x + 2y) + 10x - 8y$

23) $(-2x) - 7 + 15x + 3$

24) $3(x + 1) + 12(x - 1)$

Simplifying Polynomial Expressions

✎ Simplify each polynomial.

1) $(x^2 + 1) - (4 + x^2)$

2) $(23x^3 - 10x^2) - (4x^2 - 9x^3)$

3) $4x^5 - 5x^6 + 5x^5 - 16x^6 + 3\,x^6$

4) $(-3x^5 + 9 - 4x) + (8x^4 + 5x + 5\,x^5)$

5) $10x^2 - 5x^4 + 12x^3 - 20x^4 + 10x^3$

6) $-6x^2 + 5x^2 + 7x^3 + 16 + 32$

7) $5x^3 + 1 + 4x^2 - 3x - 10x$

8) $14x^2 - 6x^3 - 2x(2x^2 + x)$

9) $(2x^4 - x) - (2x - x^4)$

10) $(10x^3 + 2x^4) - (3x^4 - x^3)$

11) $(12 + 2x^3) + (4x^3 + 4)$

12) $(5x^2 - 3) + (x^2 - 3x^3)$

Answers of Worksheets – Chapter 5

Translate Phrases into an Algebraic Statement

1) x – 10

2) 15/x

3) x + 40

4) $\frac{x}{-10}$

5) 52 – x

6) 2x – 35

7) $5(x + (-12))$

8) $\frac{50}{-6x}$

The Distributive Property

1) – 12x + 48

2) 2x + 4

3) 6x – 3

4) –4x + 8

5) 4x + 20

6) – 12x + 16

7) 12x – 6

8) – 12x -12

9) –x +11

10) $- 16x^2 - 7x$

11) $-27x + 5$

12) – 5x – 8

Evaluating One Variable

1) 8

2) -6

3) -3

4) -13

5) 2

6) 32

7) 2

8) 5

9) -14

10) 10

Evaluating Two Variables

1) 14

2) 12

3) 9

4) 24

5) 22

6) –20

7) 69

8) 6

Expressions and Variables

1) – 100

2) -3

3) – 25

4) 48

5) 18

6) 55

7) – 8

8) 6

9) 33

10) 28

11) –21

12) 7

13) -14

14) 56

15) 53

16) 306

Combining like Terms

1) $18x - 12$

2) $6x-12$

3) $5 + 2x$

4) $3x + 3$

5) $24 - 18x$

6) $17x + 12$

7) $4x - 6$

8) $6x - 4y$

9) $-15x^3$

10) $-9x^2 - 3$

11) $10x^2 + 8$

12) $-18x - 48$

13) $11x^2 + 4x$

14) $-6x^2 + 16x$

15) $4x^2 - 7x$

16) $-20x +12$

17) $-9x + 12$

18) $64x - 12$

19) $2x + 16$

20) $-x -3$

21) $3x - 3y$

22) $4x + 6y$

23) $13x - 4$

24) $15x - 9$

Simplifying Polynomial Expressions

1) -3

2) $32x^3 - 14x^2$

3) $-18x^6 + 9x^5$

4) $2x^5 + 8x^4 + x + 9$

5) $-25x^4 + 22x^3 + 10x^2$

6) $7x^3 - x^2 + 48$

7) $5x^3 + 4x^2 - 13x + 1$

8) $-10x^3 + 12x^2$

9) $3x^4 - 3x$

10) $-x^4 + 11x^3$

11) $6x^3 + 16$

12) $-3x^3 + 6x^2 - 3$

Chapter 6: Equations and Inequalities

Topics that you'll learn in this chapter:

✓ One, Two, and Multi – Step Equations

✓ Graphing Single– Variable Inequalities

✓ One, Two, and Multi – Step Inequalities

✓ Solving Systems of Equations by Substitution and Elimination

✓ Finding Slope and Writing Linear Equations

✓ Graphing Lines Using Slope– Intercept and Standard Form

✓ Graphing Linear Inequalities

✓ Finding Midpoint and Distance of Two Points

"The study of mathematics, like the Nile, begins in minuteness but ends in magnificence." – Charles Caleb Colton

One–Step Equations

✍ Solve each equation.

1) $x + 6 = 16$

2) $42 = (-6) + x$

3) $5x = (-50)$

4) $(-81) = (-9x)$

5) $(-6) = 4 + x$

6) $3 + x = (-4)$

7) $10x = (-110)$

8) $12 = x + 6$

9) $(-25) + x = (-20)$

10) $6x = (-36)$

11) $x - 18 = (-20)$

12) $x - 9 = (-24)$

13) $(-30) = x - 25$

14) $(-7x) = 49$

15) $(-66) = (6x)$

16) $x - 10 = 30$

17) $6x = 30$

18) $36 = (-9x)$

19) $2x = 68$

20) $25x = 500$

Two–Step Equations

✎ **Solve each equation.**

1) $3(2 + x) = 9$

2) $(-6)(x - 3) = 42$

3) $(-10)(2x - 3) = (-10)$

4) $4(1 + x) = -12$

5) $14(2x + 1) = 42$

6) $6(3x + 2) = 42$

7) $3(7 + 2x) = (-60)$

8) $(-10)(2x - 3) = 48$

9) $2(x + 5) = 30$

10) $\frac{2x - 6}{4} = 2$

11) $(-24) = \frac{x + 3}{6}$

12) $110 = (-5)(x - 2)$

13) $\frac{x}{5} - 8 = 2$

14) $-15 = 9 + \frac{x}{6}$

15) $\frac{12 + x}{4} = (-10)$

16) $(-2)(6 + 2x) = (-100)$

17) $(-5x) + 10 = 30$

18) $\frac{x + 6}{5} = (-5)$

19) $\frac{x + 36}{5} = (-5)$

20) $(-8) + \frac{x}{4} = (-12)$

Multi–Step Equations

✎ Solve each equation.

1) $-(3-2x) = 7$

2) $-18 = -(3x + 12)$

3) $5x - 15 = (-x) + 3$

4) $-225 = (-3x) - 12x$

5) $4(1 + 2x) + 2x = -16$

6) $4x - 10 = 3 + x - 5 + x$

7) $10 - 2x = (-32) - 2x + 2x$

8) $7 - 3x - 3x = 3 - 3x$

9) $26 + 11x + x = (-30) + 4$

10) $(-3x) - 8(-1 + 5x) = 352$

11) $36 = (-6x) - 2 + 2$

12) $35 = 2x - 14 + 5x$

13) $5(1 + 5x) = -495$

14) $-40 = (-4x) - 6x$

15) $x + 5 = (-7) + 5x$

16) $5x - 8 = 8x + 4$

17) $10 = -(x - 8)$

18) $(-18) - 6x = 6(1 + 3x)$

19) $x + 2 = -3(6 + 3x)$

20) $5 = 1 - 2x + 4$

Graphing Single–Variable Inequalities

✎ Draw a graph for each inequality.

1) $4 \geq x$

2) $x < -2$

3) $-3 < x$

4) $-x \geq 1$

5) $x > 2$

6) $-0.5 \leq x$

One–Step Inequalities

 Solve each inequality and graph it.

1) $x + 3 \geq 9$

-10 -9 -8 -7 -6 -5 -4 -3 -2 -1 0 1 2 3 4 5 6 7 8 9 10

2) $x - 7 \leq 4$

-10 -9 -8 -7 -6 -5 -4 -3 -2 -1 0 1 2 3 4 5 6 7 8 9 10

3) $-4x < 2$

-10 -9 -8 -7 -6 -5 -4 -3 -2 -1 0 1 2 3 4 5 6 7 8 9 10

4) $-x + 5 > -8$

-10 -9 -8 -7 -6 -5 -4 -3 -2 -1 0 1 2 3 4 5 6 7 8 9 10

5) $x + 5 \geq -11$

-10 -9 -8 -7 -6 -5 -4 -3 -2 -1 0 1 2 3 4 5 6 7 8 9 10

6) $6x < 12$

-10 -9 -8 -7 -6 -5 -4 -3 -2 -1 0 1 2 3 4 5 6 7 8 9 10

7) $5x > -20$

-10 -9 -8 -7 -6 -5 -4 -3 -2 -1 0 1 2 3 4 5 6 7 8 9 10

Two–Step Inequalities

✍️ Solve each inequality and graph it.

1) $3x - 4 \leq 5$

2) $2x - 2 \leq 6$

3) $4x - 4 \leq 8$

4) $3x + 6 \geq 12$

5) $6x - 5 \geq 19$

6) $2x - 4 \leq 6$

7) $8x - 4 \leq 4$

8) $6x + 4 \leq 10$

9) $5x + 4 \leq 9$

10) $7x - 4 \leq 3$

11) $4x - 19 < 19$

12) $2x - 3 < 21$

13) $7 + 4x \geq 19$

14) $9 + 4x < 21$

15) $3 + 2x \geq 19$

16) $6 + 4x < 22$

Multi–Step Inequalities

✍️ Solve each inequality.

1) $\frac{9x}{7} - 7 < 2$

2) $\frac{4x + 8}{2} \leq 12$

3) $\frac{3x - 8}{7} > 1$

4) $-3(x - 7) > 21$

5) $4 + \frac{x}{3} < 7$

6) $\frac{2x + 6}{4} \leq 10$

Solving Systems of Equations by Substitution

Solve each system of equation by substitution.

1) $-3x + 3y = 3$

$$x + y = 3$$

2) $-10x + 2y = -6$

$$3x - 8y = 24$$

3) $y = -6$

$$15x - 10y = 75$$

4) $2y = -6x + 10$

$$10x - 8y = -6$$

5) $3x - 2y = 5$

$$3y = 3x - 3$$

6) $2x + 3y = 5$

$$3x + y = -3$$

7) $x + 10y = 6$

$$x + 5y = 1$$

8) $2x + 4y = 16$

$$x - 4, y = -1$$

Solving Systems of Equations by Elimination

✎ Solve each system of equation by elimination.

1) $-5x + y = -5$

$$-y = -6x + 6$$

2) $-6x - 2y = -2$

$$2x - 3y = 8$$

3) $5x - 4y = 8$

$$-6x + y = -21$$

4) $10x - 4y = -24$

$$-x - 20y = -18$$

5) $25x + 3y = -13$

$$12x - 6y = -36$$

6) $x - 8y = -7$

$$6x + 4y = 10$$

7) $-6x + 16y = 4$

$$5x + y = 11$$

8) $2x + 3y = 10$

$$4x + 6y = -20$$

Systems of Equations Word Problems

✐ Solve.

1) A school of 210 students went on a field trip. They took 15 vehicles, some vans and some minibuses. Find the number of vans and the number of minibuses they took if each van holds 8 students and each minibus hold 18 students.

2) The difference of two numbers is 14. Their sum is 50. Find the numbers.

3) A farmhouse shelters 15 animals, some are pigs, and some are gooses. Altogether there are 48 legs. How many of each animal are there?

4) The sum of the digits of a certain two–digit number is 9. Reversing it's increasing the number by 9. What is the number?

5) The difference of two numbers is 5. Their sum is 19. Find the numbers.

Graphing Lines of Equations

✎ **Sketch the graph of each line**

1) $y = 3x - 2$

2) $y = -\frac{1}{4}x + \frac{2}{5}$

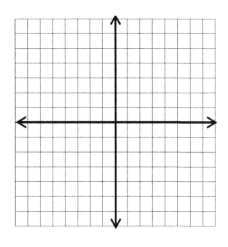

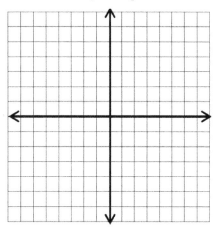

3) $4x - 2y = 6$

4) $-x - y = 3$

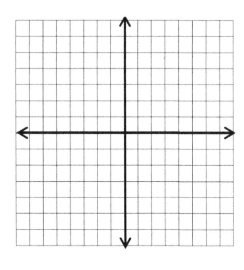

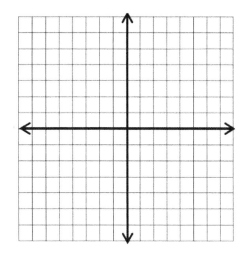

Graphing Linear Inequalities

✎ Sketch the graph of each linear inequality.

1) $y \leq 2x - \frac{2}{3}$

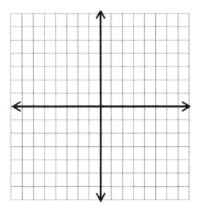

2) $-2x - 3y > \frac{1}{2}$

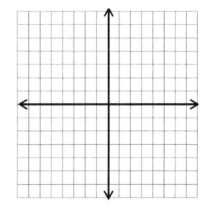

4) $-\frac{1}{2}x + 3y \geq -5$

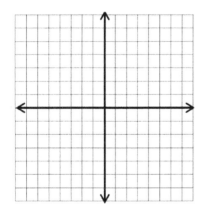

5) $3x - \frac{2}{7}y < 4$

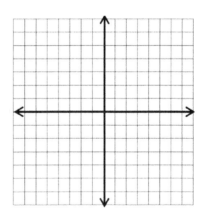

Finding Distance of Two Points

✏️ **Find the midpoint of the line segment with the given endpoints.**

1) $(1, -3), (2, -2)$

7) $(1, 2), (-1, -2)$

2) $(0, 2), (-1, -4)$

8) $(7, 0.5), (-2, 0)$

3) $(2, 5), (3, -5)$

9) $(-4, 6), (-3, -1)$

4) $(1.5, 2.5), (3, 5)$

10) $(3.1, -2.7), (-1.2, 3)$

5) $(-2, 0), (0, -2)$

11) $(5.2, 6.3), (4, -2)$

6) $(5, -4), (2, 5)$

12) $(4, 6), (-2, 4)$

✏️ **Find the distance between each pair of points.**

1) $(4, -1), (2, -1)$

7) $(0, 6), (1, 3)$

2) $(5, -2), (3, 4)$

8) $(9, 8), (-4, -3)$

3) $(-3, -7), (-1, 2)$

9) $(2, 3), (-2, -3)$

4) $(7, -3), (-5, 0)$

10) $(-4, -2), (4, 2)$

5) $(-8, -5), (-3, -5)$

11) $(-12, -15), (-7, -9)$

6) $(11, 1.5), (-2, -8)$

12) $(3, -4), (0, 0)$

Answers of Worksheets – Chapter 6

One–Step Equations

1) 10	6) − 7	11) − 2	16) 40
2) 48	7) − 11	12) − 15	17) 5
3) − 10	8) -6	13) 5	18) − 4
4) 9	9) 5	14) -4	19) 34
5) − 10	10) − 6	15) -11	20) 20

Two–Step Equations

1) 1	6) $\frac{5}{3}$	11) − 147	16) 22
2) -4	7) $-\frac{81}{6}$	12) − 20	17) 4
3) 2	8) 0.9	13) 50	18) − 31
4) -4	9) 10	14) -144	19) − 61
5) 1	10) 7	15) − 28	20) − 16

Multi–Step Equations

1) 5	6) 4	11) − 6	16) -4
2) 2	7) 21	12) 7	17) 1 8
3) 2	8) $\frac{4}{3}$	13) -20	18) − 1
4) 15	9) 7	14) 4	19) − 2
5) − 2	10) − 8	15) 3	20) 0

Graphing Single–Variable Inequalities

 1) $4 \geq x$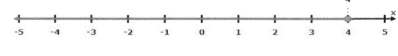

 2) $x < -2$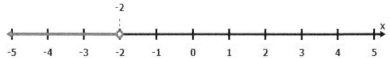

3) $-3 < x$

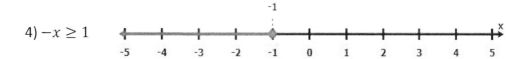

4) $-x \geq 1$

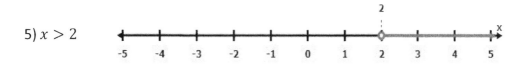

5) $x > 2$

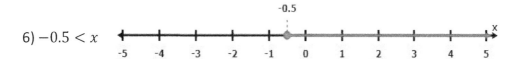

6) $-0.5 < x$

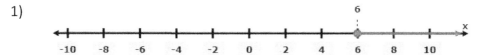

One–Step Inequalities

1)

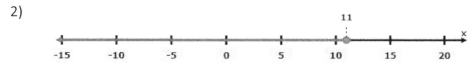

2)

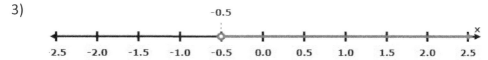

3)

4)

5)

6)

7)

Two–Step inequalities

1) $x \leq 3$ 5) $x \geq 4$ 9) $x \leq 1$ 13) $x \geq 3$

2) $x \leq 4$ 6) $x \leq 5$ 10) $x \leq 1$ 14) $x < 3$

3) $x \leq 3$ 7) $x \leq 1$ 11) $x < 9.5$ 15) $x \geq 8$

4) $x \geq 2$ 8) $x \leq 1$ 12) $x < 12$ 16) $x < 4$

Multi–Step inequalities.

1) $x < 7$ 3) $x > 5$ 5) $x < 9$

2) $x \leq 4$ 4) $x < 0$ 6) $x \leq 17$

Solving Systems of Equations by Substitution

1) (0, 1)   4) (1, 2)   7) (-4, 1)

2) (0, −3)   5) (3, 2)   8) $(5, \frac{3}{2})$

3) (1, −6)   6) (-2, 3)

Solving Systems of Equations by Elimination

1) (−1, 0)   4) (-2, 1)   7) (2, 1)

2) (1, −2)   5) (−1, 4)   8) No solution

3) (4, 3)   6) (1, 1)

Systems of Equations Word Problems

1) There are 6 van and 9 minibuses.

2) 32 and 18

3) There are 9 pigs and 6 gooses.

4) 45

5) 12 and 7.

Writing Linear Equations

1) $y = -\frac{1}{2}x + 5.5$ 2) $y = 3x + 7$

3) $y = \frac{1}{4}x + \frac{7}{8}$

4) $y = -\frac{1}{6}x - \frac{23}{8}$

5) $y = -7x - 7$

6) $y = -3x + 15$

7) $y = \frac{1}{2}x - \frac{1}{2}$

8) $y = -\frac{1}{3}x + \frac{4}{5}$

9) $y = 3x - 15$

10) $y = 5$

11) $y = 2x$

12) $y = x - 2$

Graphing Lines Using Slope–Intercept Form

1)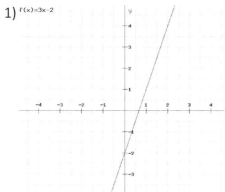

2)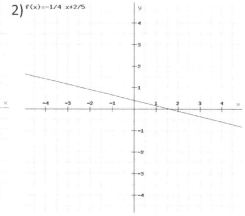

3)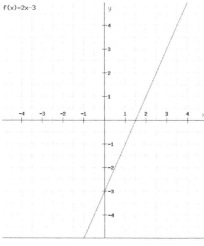

4)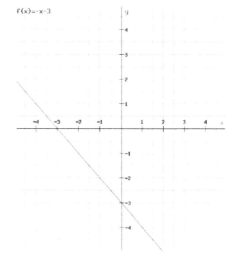

Graphing Linear Inequalities

1)

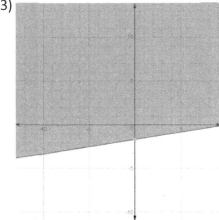

2)

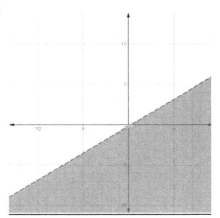

3)

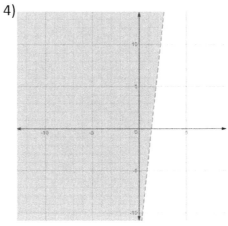

4)

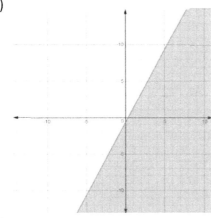

Finding Midpoint

1) $(1.5, -2.5)$

2) $(-1, -1)$

3) $(2.5, 0)$

4) $(2.25, 3.75)$

5) $(-2, -2)$

6) $(3.5, 0.5)$

7) $(0, 0)$

8) $(2.5, 0.25)$

9) $(-3.5, 2.5)$

10) $(0.95, 0.15)$

11) $(4.60, 2.15)$

12) $(1, 5)$

Finding Distance of Two Points

1) 2

2) 6.32

3) 9.22

4) 12.37

5) 5

6) 16.1

7) 3.16

8) 17.03

9) 7.21

10) 8.94

11) 7.81

12) 5

Chapter 7: Polynomials

Topics that you'll learn in this chapter:

- ✓ Classifying Polynomials

- ✓ Writing Polynomials in Standard Form

- ✓ Simplifying Polynomials

- ✓ Adding and Subtracting Polynomials

- ✓ Multiplying and Dividing Monomials

- ✓ Multiplying a Polynomial and a Monomial

- ✓ Multiplying Binomials

- ✓ Factoring Trinomials

- ✓ Operations with Polynomials

Mathematics – the unshaken Foundation of Sciences, and the plentiful Fountain of Advantage to human affairs. — Isaac Barrow

Classifying Polynomials

✎ Name each polynomial by degree and number of terms.

1) $x + 4$

2) -8

3) $-5x^4$

4) $9x^2 - 8x^3$

5) $2x - 1$

6) $8x^5$

7) $9x^2 - x$

8) $-5x^4 + 4x^3 - x^2 - 6x$

9) $x - 6x^2 + 4x^3 - 5x^4$

10) $4x^6 + 5x^5 - x^4$

11) $-4 + 2x^2 + x$

12) $9x^6 - 8$

13) $7x^5 + 10x^4 + 3x + 9x^7$

14) $4x^6 + 3x^2 - 5x^4$

✎ Write each polynomial in standard form

1) $x^2 - 4x^3$

2) $x^2 + x - x3$

3) $12 - 7x + 9x^4$

4) $x^2 + 12x - 8x3$

5) $x(x + 2) - (x + 2)$

6) $x^2 + x + 13 - 8x^2 - 4x$

7) $10x^5 + x^3 - 3x^5 - 4x^3$

8) $x (x + 6 - 8x^2)$

9) $x (x^5 + 2x^3)$

10) $(x + 4)(x + 2)$

11) $(x + 3)^2$

12) $(x - 5) (2x + 3)$

13) $x(1 + 3x^2 + 2x)$

14) $x (2 - x + 2x^3)$

Simplifying Polynomials

✎ Simplify each expression.

1) $5 - 3x^2 + 7x^2 - 2x^3 + 6$

2) $23x^5 - 3x^5 + 7x^2 - 23x^5$

3) $(-2)(x^6 + 9) - 6(10 + x^6)$

4) $3(2x^2 + 4x^2 + 3x^3) - 9x^3 + 17$

5) $3 - 6x^2 + 8x^2 - 13x^3 + 26$

6) $x^2 - 2x + 3x^3 + 16x - 20x$

7) $(x - 6)(3x - 5)$

8) $(12x + y)^2$

9) $(12x^3 + 28x^2 + 10x + 4) \div (x + 2)$

10) $(2x + 12x^2 - 2) \div (2x + 1)$

11) $(x^3 - 1) + (4x^3 - 3x^3)$

12) $(x - 2)(x + 3)$

13) $(2x + 6)(2x - 6)$

14) $(x^2 - 3x) + (5x - 5 - 8x^2)$

Adding and Subtracting Polynomials

1) $(4x^3 + 8) - (9 + 5x^3)$

2) $(x^3 + 8) + (x^3 - 8)$

3) $(2x^2 + 5x^3) - (5x^3 + 9)$

4) $(5x^2 - 2x) + (3x - 6x^2)$

5) $(12x - 7x^3) - (4x^3 + 4x)$

6) $(2x^3 - x^2) - (3x^2 - 4x^3)$

7) $(x^2 - 8) + (8x^2 - 3x^3)$

8) $(x^3 + x^4) - (x^4 + 5x^3)$

9) $(-10x^4 + 12x^5 + x^3) + (14x^3 + 10x^5 + 16x^4)$

10) $(12x^2 - 6x^5 - 2x) + (-10x^2 + 11x^5 - 9x)$

11) $(35 + 8x^5 - 4x^2) + (7x^4 + 2x^5) - (27 - 4x^4)$

12) $(4x^5 - 3x^3 - 3x) + (3x + 10x^4 - 12) + (2x^2 + x^3 + 10)$

Multiplying Monomials

1) $4xy^2z \times 3z^2$

2) $6xy \times 2x^2y$

3) $6pq^3 \times (-3p^4q)$

4) $6s^4t^2 \times st^5$

5) $12p^3 \times (-4p^4)$

6) $-4p^2q^3r \times 4pq^2r^3$

7) $(-4)(-24a^6b)$

8) $2u^4v^2 \times (-10u^2v^3)$

9) $5u^3 \times (-3u)$

10) $-8xy^2 \times 4x^2y$

11) $24y^2z^3 \times (-y^2z)$

12) $10a^2bc^2 \times 3abc^2$

Multiply and Divide Monomials

1) $(8x^4y^6)(4x^3y^4)$

2) $\dfrac{60x^5y^8}{40x^7y^{11}}$

3) $(14x^4)(4x^9)$

4) $\dfrac{60x^{12}y^9}{20x^6y^7}$

5) $(-2x^{-4}y^2)^5$

6) $\dfrac{85x^{18}y^7}{5x^9y^2}$

7) $(12x^2y^9)(6x^9y^{12})$

8) $\dfrac{200x^3y^8}{20x^3y^7}$

9) $(3x^{-5}y^4)^{-2}$

10) $\dfrac{-18x^{17}y^{13}}{3x^6y^9}$

11) $(-5x^{-3}y^{-1})(-4x^{-4}y^3)$

12) $\dfrac{-81x^8y^{10}}{9x^3y^7}$

Multiply a Polynomial and a Monomial

1) $4(3x - 4y)$

2) $9x(3x + 5y)$

3) $8x(8x - 5)$

4) $12x(3x + 9)$

5) $12x(2x - 2y)$

6) $3x(5x - 6y)$

7) $x(2x^2 - 3x + 8)$

8) $12x(2x + 4y)$

9) $30(2x^2 - 8x - 5)$

10) $6x^3(3x^2 - x + 1)$

11) $8x^2(4x^2 - 5xy + y^2)$

12) $x^2(3x^2 - 5x + 10)$

13) $2x^3(x^2 + 6x - 2)$

14) $4x(3x^2 - 4xy + 2y^2)$

Multiply Binomials

1) $(x - 2)(5x + 2)$

2) $(3x - 2)(x + 5)$

3) $(x + 2)(x + 8)$

4) $(x^2 + 3)(x^2 - 3)$

5) $(x - 3)(x + 6)$

6) $(x - 6)(2x + 6)$

7) $(x - 4)(3x - 3)$

8) $(x - 5)(x - 4)$

9) $(x + 5)(2x + 5)$

10) $(x - 6)(3x + 6)$

11) $(x - 8)(x + 8)$

12) $(x - 4)(4x + 8)$

13) $(2x - 6)(2x + 6)$

14) $(x + 7)(x - 2)$

15) $(x - 7)(x + 7)$

16) $(4x + 4)(4x - 3)$

Factor Trinomials

1) $x^2 - 6x + 8$

2) $x^2 - 5x - 14$

3) $x^2 - 10x - 24$

4) $2x^2 + 3x - 9$

5) $x^2 - 16x + 48$

6) $x^2 + 3x - 18$

7) $3x^2 + 7x + 2$

8) $x^2 - 3x - 10$

9) $8x^2 + 22x - 6$

10) $x^2 + 22x + 121$

11) $64x^2 + 16xy + 4y^2$

12) $6x^2 - 20x + 16$

13) $x^2 - 12x + 36$

14) $25x^2 + 20x + 4$

Operations with Polynomials

1) $2x^2(4x - 3)$

2) $4x^2(6x - 3)$

3) $-5(5x - 3)$

4) $4x^3(-4x + 6)$

5) $7(7x + 2)$

6) $9(3x + 7)$

7) $4(7x + 1)$

8) $-6x^4(x - 4)$

9) $8(x^2 - 2x + 3)$

10) $2(4x^2 - 2x + 1)$

11) $2(4x^2 + 3x - 2)$

12) $7x(2x^2 + 3x + 8)$

13) $(8x + 1)(2x - 1)$

14) $(x + 5)(3x - 5)$

15) $(6x - 4)(3x - 6)$

16) $(x - 4)(3x + 6)$

Answers of Worksheets – Chapter 7

Classifying Polynomials

1) Linear monomial

2) Constant monomial

3) Quantic monomial

4) cubic binomial

5) linear binomial

6) Quantic monomial

7) Quadratic binomial

8) Quartic polynomial with four terms

9) Quartic polynomial with four terms

10) Sixth degree trinomial

11) Quadratic trinomial

12) Sixth degree binomial

13) Seventh degree polynomial with four terms

14) Sixth degree trinomial

Writing Polynomials in Standard Form

1) $-4x^3 + x^2$

2) $-x^3 + x^2 + x$

3) $9x^4 - 7x + 12$

4) $-8x^3 + x^2 + 12x$

5) $x^2 + x - 2$

6) $-7x^2 - 3x + 13$

7) $7x^5 - 3x^3$

8) $-8x^3 + x^2 + 6x$

9) $x^6 + 2x^4$

10) $x^2 + 6x + 8$

11) $x^2 + 6x + 9$

12) $2x^2 - 7x - 15$

13) $3x^3 + 2x^2 + x$

14) $2x^4 - x^2 + 2x$

Simplifying Polynomials

1) $-2x^3 + 4x^2 + 11$

2) $-3x^3 + 7x^2$

3) $-8x^6 - 78$

4) $18x^2 + 17$

5) $-13x^3 + 2x^2 + 29$

6) $3x^3 + x^2 - 6x$

7) $3x^2 - 23x + 30$

8) $144x^2 + 24xy + y^2$

9) $12x^2 + 4x + 2$

10) $6x - 2$

11) $2x^3 - 1$

12) $x^2 + x - 6$

13) $4x^2 - 36$

14) $-7x^2 + 2x - 5$

Adding and Subtracting Polynomials

1) $-x^3 - 1$

2) $2x^3$

3) $2x^2 - 9$

4) $-x^2 + x$

5) $-11x^3 + 8x$

6) $6x^3 - 4x^2$

7) $-3x^3 + 9x^2 - 8$

8) $-4x^3$

9) $22x^5 + 6x^4 + 15x^3$

10) $5x^5 + 2x^2 - 11x$

11) $10x^5 + 11x^4 - 4x^2 + 8$

12) $4x^5 + 10x^4 - 2x^3 + 2x^2 - 2$

Multiply Monomials

1) $12xy^2z^3$

2) $12x^3y^2$

3) $-18p^5q^4$

4) $6s^5t^7$

5) $-48p^7$

6) $-16p^3q^5r^4$

7) $96a^6b$

8) $-20u^6v^5$

9) $-15u^4$

10) $-32x^3y^3$

11) $-24y^4z^4$

12) $30a^3b^2c^4$

Multiply and Divide Monomials

1) $32x^7y^{10}$

2) $1.5x^{-2}y^{-3}$

3) $56x^{13}$

4) $3x^6y^2$

5) $-32x^{-20}y^{10}$

6) $17x^9y^5$

7) $72x^{11}y^{21}$

8) $10y$

9) $\frac{1}{9}x^{10}y^{-8}$

10) $-6x^{11}y^4$

11) $(20x^{-7}y^2)$

12) $-9x^5y^3$

Multiply a Polynomial and a Monomial

1) $12x - 16y$

2) $72x^2 + 45xy$

3) $64x^2 - 40x$

4) $36x^2 + 108x$

5) $24x^2 - 24xy$

6) $15x^2 - 18xy$

7) $2x^3 - 3x^2 + 8x$

8) $24x^2 + 48xy$

9) $60x^2 - 240x - 150$

10) $18x^5 - 6x^4 + 6x^3$

11) $32x^4 - 40x^3y + 8y^2x^2$

12) $3x^4 - 5x^3 + 10x^2$

13) $2x^5 + 12x^4 - 4x^3$

14) $12x^3 - 16x^2y + 8xy^2$

Multiplying Binomials

1) $5x^2 - 8x - 4$

2) $3x^2 + 13x - 10$

3) $x^2 + 10x + 16$

4) $x^4 - 9$

5) $x^2 + 3x - 18$

6) $2x^2 - 6x - 36$

7) $3x^2 - 15x + 12$

8) $x^2 - 9x + 20$

9) $2x^2 + 15x + 25$

10) $3x^2 - 13x - 36$

11) $x^2 - 64$

12) $3x^2 - 13x - 32$

13) $4x^2 - 36$

14) $x^2 + 5x - 14$

15) $x^2 - 49$

16) $16x^2 + 4x - 12$

Factoring Trinomials

1) $(x - 4)(x - 2)$

2) $(x + 2)(x - 7)$

3) $(x + 2)(x - 12)$

4) $(x + 3)(2x - 3)$

5) $(x - 14)(x - 2)$

6) $(x - 3)(x + 6)$

7) $(3x + 1)(x + 2)$

8) $(x - 5)(x + 2)$

9) $(4x - 1)(2x + 6)$

10) $(x + 11)(x + 11)$

11) $(8x + 2y)(8x + 2y)$

12) $(2x - 4)(3x - 4)$

13) $(x - 6)(x - 6)$

14) $(5x + 2)(5x + 2)$

Operations with Polynomials

1) $8x^3 - 6x^2$

2) $24x^3 - 12x^2$

3) $-25x + 15$

4) $-16x^4 + 24x^3$

5) $49x + 14$

6) $18x + 63$

7) $28x + 4$

8) $-6x^5 + 24x^4$

9) $8x^2 - 16x + 24$

10) $8x^2 - 4x + 2$

11) $8x^2 + 6x - 4$

12) $14x^3 + 21x^2 + 56x$

13) $16x^2 - 6x - 1$

14) $3x^2 + 10x - 25$

15) $18x^2 - 48x + 24$

16) $3x^2 - 6x - 24$

Chapter 8: Linear Functions

Topics that you'll learn in this chapter:

- ✓ Relations and Functions
- ✓ Adding and Subtracting Functions
- ✓ Multiplying and Dividing Functions
- ✓ Finding Slope and Rate of Change
- ✓ Find the X–intercept and Y–intercept
- ✓ Graphing Lines Using Slope–Intercept Form
- ✓ Graphing Lines Using Standard Form
- ✓ Writing Linear Equations
- ✓ Write an Equation from a Graph
- ✓ Equations of horizontal and vertical lines
- ✓ Equation of parallel or perpendicular lines
- ✓ Solving Quadratic Functions

Without mathematics, there's nothing you can do. Everything around you are mathematics. Everything around you are numbers." – Shakuntala Devi

Relation and Functions

⊯State the domain and range of each relation. Then determine whether each relation is a function.

1)

Function:

....

Domain:

....

Range:

....

2)

x	y
2	2
0	0
-1	-1
4	-1
5	1

Function:

....

Domain:

....

Range:

....

3)

Function:

....

Domain:

....

Range: ....

4) $\{(2,-1),(3,-2),(0,1),(3,0),$

Function: ....

Domain:

....

Range:

....

5)

Function:

....

Domain:

....

Range:

....

6)

Function:

....

Domain:

....

Range:

....

Slope and Rate of Change

✍ Find the slope of the line through each pair of points.

1) $(4, 1), (2, 5)$

2) $(1, -6), (-5, 3)$

3) $(2, -7), (5, -8)$

4) $(12, 9), (18, 14)$

5) $(0, -3), (7, -2)$

6) $(11, -7), (13, -5)$

7) $(-3, -5), (-11, -1)$

8) $(0, 0), (6, -1)$

9) $(16, -9), (-4, 4)$

10) $(-8, 6), (-8, 2)$

11) $(-12, -7), (-4, -13)$

12) $(-14, 0), (0, -14)$

✍ Write the slope–intercept form of the equation of the line through the given points.

1) Through: $(5, 3), (7, 2)$

2) Through: $(-4, -5), (-3, -2)$

3) Through: $(0.4, 1), (2, 1.4)$

4) Through: $(7, -3), (2.5, 1)$

5) Through: $(-1, 0), (-2, 7)$

6) Through: $(7, -6), (2, 9)$

7) Through: $(9, 4), (7, 3)$

8) Through: $(-0.5, 1), (5.5, -1)$

9) Through: $(4, -3), (8, 9)$

10) Through: $(1, 5), (-2, 5)$

11) Through: $(2, 4), (-1, -2)$

12) Through: $(8, 6), (0, -2)$

Find the value of b: The line that passes through each pair of points has the given slope.

1) $(3, -2), (1, b), m = 1$

2) $(b, -6), (-3, 8), m = -1\frac{2}{5}$

3) $(-3, b), (3, 7), m = \frac{1}{3}$

4) $(0, 2), (b, 5), m = -\frac{1}{3}$

✎ Write the slope intercept form of the equation of each line

1)

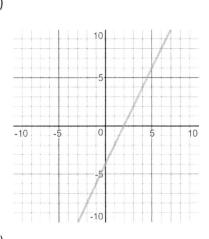

2)

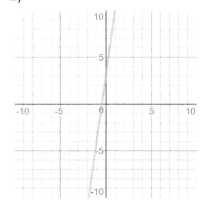

3)

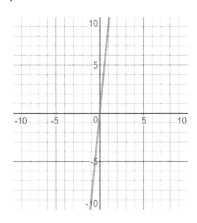

4)

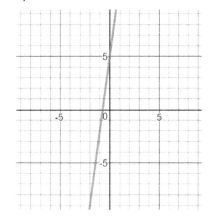

Rate of change

✍ **What is the average rate of change of the function?**

1) $f(x) = 2x^2 + 3$, from $x = 3$ to $x = 7$?

2) $f(x) = -x^2 - 2$, from $x = 0$ to $x = 2$?

3) $f(x) = x^3 + 1$, from $x = 1$ to $x = 3$?

x and *y* intercepts

✍ **Find the** x **and** y **intercepts for the following equations.**

1) $3x + 2y = 12$ 2) $y = x + 7$ 3) $3x = y + 15$

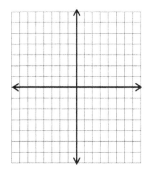 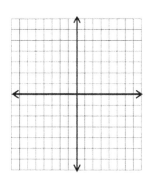 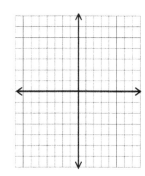

4) $x + y = 0$ 5) $7x - 3y = 5$ 6) $5y - 4x + 8 = 0$

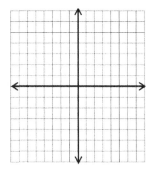 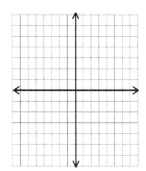 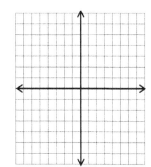

Slope–intercept Form

✎ Write the slope–intercept form of the equation of each line.

1) $-12x + y = 5$

2) $-3(5x + y) = 45$

3) $-7x - 14y = -42$

4) $6x + 25 = -4y$

5) $x - 2y = 8$

6) $21x - 15y = -9$

7) $32x - 16y = -64$

8) $9x - 6y + 27 = 0$

9) $-\frac{2}{7}y = -3x + 1$

10) $7 - y - 3x = 0$

11) $-y = -3x - 8$

12) $8x + 4y = -16$

13) $2(x + y + 5) = 0$

14) $y - 5 = x + 6$

15) $4(y + 3) = 5(x - 3)$

16) $\frac{2}{3}y + \frac{1}{3}x + \frac{4}{3} =$

Point–slope Form

Find the slope of the following lines. Name a point on each line.

1) $y = 3(x + 2)$

2) $y + 5 = \dfrac{2}{3}(x - 2)$

3) $y + 1 = -2.5x$

4) $y - 5 = \dfrac{1}{2}(x - 4)$

5) $y + 2 = 1.4(x + 2)$

6) $y - 7 = -4x$

7) $y - 10 = -4(x - 6)$

8) $y + 15 = 0$

9) $y + 8 = 3(x + 1)$

10) $y - 11 = -7(x - 3)$

Write an equation in point–slope form for the line that passes through the given point with the slope provided.

11) $(2, -1), m = 5$

12) $(-2, 4), m = \dfrac{1}{2}$

13) $(0, -8), m = -1$

14) $(a, b), m = m$

15) $(-5, 3), m = 5$

16) $(2, 0), m = -6$

17) $(-6, 8), m = \dfrac{2}{3}$

18) $(-1, 12), m = 0$

19) $\left(-\dfrac{1}{4}, 2\right), m = \dfrac{1}{8}$

20) $(0, 0), m = -4$

Equation of Parallel or Perpendicular Lines

✍️ *Write an equation of the line that passes through the given*

point and is parallel to the given line.

1) $(-2, -4), 2x + 3y = -6$

2) $(-3, 0), y = x - 3$

3) $(-1, 0), 3y = 7x - 2$

4) $(0, 0), -2y + 6x - 15 = 0$

5) $(2, 13), y + 17 = 0$

6) $(0, 5), -8x - y = -7$

7) $(-3, -2), y = \frac{3}{4}x + 2$

8) $(-1, 3), -6x + 5y = -17$

9) $(5, -3), y = -\frac{3}{5}x - 2$

10) $(-4, -4), 9x + 12y = -24$

✍️ Write an equation of the line that passes through the given

point and is perpendicular to the given line.

11) $(-2, -5), 2x + 3y = -9$

12) $\left(-\frac{1}{2}, \frac{3}{4}\right), 3x - 9y = -24$

13) $(3, -7), y = -7$

14) $(8, -4), x = 8$

15) $(0, -4), y = \frac{1}{3}x + 5$

16) $\left(\frac{2}{5}, \frac{4}{5}\right), y = -4x - 21$

17) $(-6, 0), y = \frac{3}{2}x - 13$

18) $(1, -3), y = x + 15$

19) $(-2, -2), y = \frac{5}{4}x - 1$

20) $(0, 0), y - 7x + 6 = 0$

Graphing Lines of Equations

✍ **Sketch the graph of each line**

1) $y = 3x - 2$

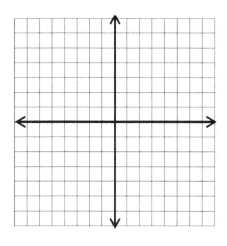

2) $y = -\frac{1}{4}x + \frac{2}{5}$

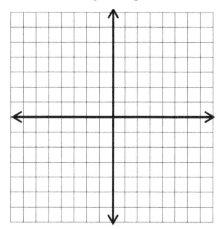

3) $4x - 2y = 6$

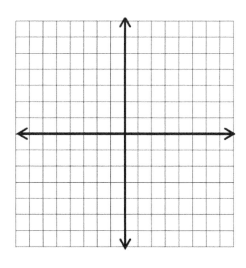

4) $-x - y = 3$

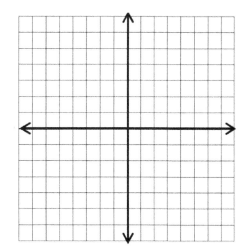

Equations of Horizontal and Vertical Lines

✎ Sketch the graph of each line.

1) $y = 2$

2) $y = 0$

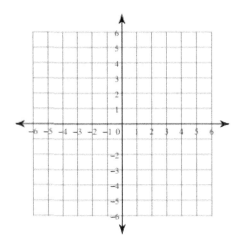
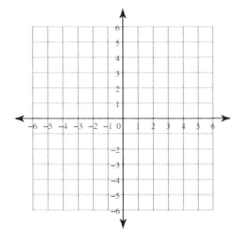

3) $x = 3$

4) $x = -4$

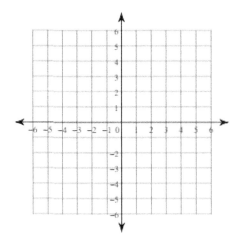
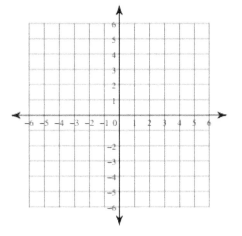

Function Notation

✎**Write in function notation.**

1) $v = 7t$

2) $r = 2p^2 + p - 1$

3) $h = 14g + 7$

4) $y = 3x - \dfrac{2}{5}$

✎**Evaluate each function.**

5) $w(x) = 5x + 2$, find $w(3)$

6) $h(n) = n^2 - 4$, find $h(-2)$

7) $h(x) = x^3 - 4$, find $h(-1)$

8) $h(m) = -3m^2 + 4m$, find $h(5)$

9) $f(n) = n^2 - n$, find $g(12)$

10) $g(x) = x^3 + 12x + 8$, find $g(0)$

11) $f(u) = 8u - 3$, find $g(^1/_4)$

12) $h(x) = 2x - 4$, find $h(a)$

13) $h(a) = -6a + 2$, find $h(2b)$

14) $k(a) = -2a + 1$, find $k(a - 3)$

15) $h(x) = x^3 + 2x^2 - 5$, find $h(x^2)$

16) $h(x) = x^2 + 2$, find $h(-\dfrac{x}{2})$

Adding and Subtracting Functions

✎*Perform the indicated operation.*

1) $h(t) = 3t - 2; g(t) = 3t + 2$

   Find $(h - g)(t)$.

2) $g(a) = -2a^2 + 1; f(a) = a^2 - a + 4$

   Find $(g - f)(a)$.

3) $g(x) = 3x - 4; h(x) = x - 7$

   Find $g(2) - h(2)$.

4) $h(3) = -2x + 1; g(x) = 3x - 5$

   Find $(h + g)(3)$.

5) $f(x) = 4x - 2; g(x) = x^2 + x$

   Find $(f - g)(-1)$.

6) $h(n) = 3n - 3 ; g(n) = n^2 - 2n + 4$

   Find $(h + g)(a)$.

7) $g(x) = -x^2 + 5 - 2x; f(x) = 11 + 3x$

   Find $(g - f)(x)$.

8) $h(x) = x^2 - 8; g(x) = -2x^2 + x$

   Find $(h + g)(t)$.

9) $g(t) = t + 7; f(t) = -2t^2 + t$

   Find $(g - f)(u + 1)$.

10) $k(x) = -2x + 9; h(x) = -x^2 + 2x - 4$

   Find $(k + h)(t - 5)$.

Multiplying and Dividing Functions

✎*Perform the indicated operation.*

1) $g(a) = 3a - 2; h(a) = 5a - 1$

   Find $(g.h)(-2)$

2) $f(x) = x^3 - 2x^2; g(x) = 3x - 1$

   Find $(f.g)(x)$

3) $g(t) = \frac{1}{2}t^2 + \frac{1}{2}; h(t) = 2t - 6$

   Find $(h.g)(-\frac{1}{2})$

4) $k(n) = n^2 - n; h(n) = 2n^2 + 2$

   Find $(k.h)(1)$

5) $f(a) = 11a - 16; g(a) = 5a + 12$

   Find $(\frac{f}{g})(-2)$

6) $f(x) = x - 1; g(x) = x^2 - 1$

   Find $(\frac{g}{f})(x)$

7) $h(a) = -2a; g(a) = -a^2 - a$

   Find $(\frac{h}{g})(a)$

8) $f(t) = -a + 2; g(t) = a^3 - 1$

   Find $(\frac{2f}{g})(a)$

Composition of Functions

✍Using $f(x) = 3x - 7$, and $g(x) = -x + 1$, find:

1) $f(g(1))$

2) $f(f(0))$

3) $g(f(-5))$

✍Using $f(x) = -2x + 5$, and $g(x) = x - 4$, find:

4) $f(g(-3))$

5) $g(g(2))$

6) $g(f(\frac{1}{2}))$

✍Using $f(x) = 5x - 2a$, and $g(x) = x^2 - 3$, find:

7) $(fog)(-1) = f(g(-1))$

8) $(fof)(4)$

9) $(gof)(-1)$

✍Using $f(x) = -x + 5$, and $g(x) = x + b$, find:

10) $(fog)(x)$

11) $(fog)(x + 2)$

12) $(gof)(x^2)$

Answers of Worksheets – Chapter 8

Relation and Functions

1) No, $D_f = \{2, 4, 6, 8, 10\}$, $R_f = \{4, 8, 12, 16, 20\}$

2) Yes, $D_f = \{2, 0, -1, 4, 5\}$, $R_f = \{2, 0, -1, -1, 1\}$

3) Yes, $D_f = (-\infty, \infty)$, $R_f = \{-2, \infty)$

4) No, $D_f = \{2, 3, 0, 3, 1\}$, $R_f = \{-1, -2, 1, 0, 1\}$

5) No, $D_f = [-2, 2]$, $R_f = [-2, 3]$

6) Yes, $D_f = \{0, 3, 7, 5\}$, $R_f = \{2, 1, 4, 5\}$

Finding Slope

1) -2

2) -1.5

3) $-\frac{1}{3}$

4) $\frac{5}{6}$

5) $\frac{1}{7}$

6) 1

7) $-\frac{1}{2}$

8) $-\frac{1}{6}$

9) $-\frac{13}{20}$

10) Undefined

11) $-\frac{3}{4}$

12) -1

Writing Linear Equations

1) $y = -\frac{1}{2}x + 5.5$

2) $y = 3x + 7$

3) $y = \frac{1}{4}x + \frac{9}{10}$

4) $y = -\frac{8}{9}x + 3\frac{2}{9}$

5) $y = -7x - 7$

6) $y = -3x + 15$

7) $y = \frac{1}{2}x - \frac{1}{2}$

8) $y = -\frac{1}{3}x + \frac{5}{6}$

9) $y = 3x - 15$

10) $y = 5$

11) $y = 2x$

12) $y = x - 2$

Find the value of b

1) -4

2) 7

3) 5

4) -9

Write an equation from a graph

1) $y = 2x - 4$

2) $y = 7x + 3$

3) $y = 9x$

4) $y = 7x + 5$

Rate of change

1) 20   2) -2 3) 13

x–intercept and y–intercept

1) $y - \text{intercept} = 6$

   $x - \text{intercept} = 4$

2) $y - \text{intercept} = 7$

   $x - \text{intercept} = -7$

3) $y - \text{intercept} = -15$

   $x - \text{intercept} = 5$

4) $y - \text{intercept} = 0$

   $x - \text{intercept} = 0$

5) $y - \text{intercept} = -\dfrac{5}{3}$

   $x - \text{intercept} = \dfrac{5}{7}$

6) $y - \text{intercept} = -\dfrac{8}{5}$

   $x - \text{intercept} = 2$

Slope–intercept form

1) $y = 12x + 5$

2) $y = -5x - 15$

3) $y = -\dfrac{1}{2}x + 3$

4) $y = -\dfrac{3}{2}x - \dfrac{25}{4}$

5) $y = \dfrac{x}{2} - 4$

6) $y = \dfrac{7}{5}x + \dfrac{3}{5}$

7) $y = 2x + 4$

8) $y = \dfrac{3}{2}x + \dfrac{9}{2}$

9) $y = \dfrac{21}{2}x - \dfrac{7}{2}$

10) $y = -3x + 7$

11) $y = 3x + 8$

12) $y = -2x - 4$

13) $y = -x - 5$

14) $y = x + 11$

15) $y = \dfrac{5}{4}x - \dfrac{27}{4}$

16) $y = -\dfrac{1}{2}x - 2$

Point–slope form

1) $m = 3, (-2, 0)$

2) $m = \dfrac{2}{3}, (5, -3)$

3) 3) $m = -\dfrac{5}{2}, (0, -1)$

4) $m = \dfrac{1}{2}, (6, 6)$

5) $m = \dfrac{14}{10}, (-2, -2)$

6) $m = -4, (0, 7)$

7) $m = -4, (1, 30)$

8) $m = 0, (5, -15)$

9) $m = 3, (0, -5)$

10) $m = -7, (-2, 46)$

11) $y + 1 = 5(x - 2)$

12) $y - 4 = \frac{1}{2}(x + 2)$

13) $y + 8 = -x$

14) $y - b = m(x - a)$

15) $y - 3 = 5(x + 5)$

16) $y = -6(x - 2)$

17) $y - 8 = \frac{2}{3}(x + 6)$

18) $y - 12 = 0$

19) $y - 2 = \frac{1}{8}\left(x + \frac{1}{4}\right)$

20) $y = -4x$

Equation of parallel or perpendicular line.

1) $y = -\frac{2}{3}x - 5\frac{1}{3}$

2) $y = x + 3$

3) $y = \frac{7}{3}x + \frac{7}{3}$

4) $y = 3x$

5) $y = 13$

6) $y = -8x + 5$

7) $y = \frac{3}{4}x + \frac{1}{4}$

8) $y = \frac{6}{5}x + \frac{21}{5}$

9) $y = -\frac{3}{5}x$

10) $y = -\frac{3}{4}x - 7$

11) $y = \frac{3}{2}x - 2$

12) $y = -3x - \frac{3}{4}$

13) $x = 3$

14) $y = -4$

15) $y = -3x - 4$

16) $y = \frac{1}{4}x + \frac{7}{10}$

17) $y = -\frac{2}{3}x - 4$

18) $y = -x - 2$

19) $y = -\frac{4}{5}x - \frac{18}{5}$

20) $y = -\frac{1}{7}x$

Equations of horizontal and vertical lines

1) $y = 2$

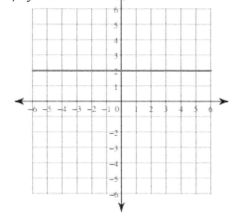

2) $y = 0$ (it is on x axes)

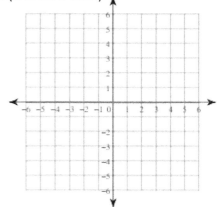

3) $x = 3$

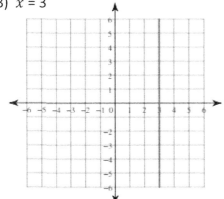

4) $x = -4$

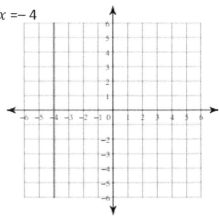

Function Notation

1) $v(t) = 7t$

2) $r(p) = 2p^2 +$
   $p - 1$

3) $h(g) = 14g + 7$

4) $f(x) = 3x - \frac{2}{5}$

5) 17

6) 0

7) -5

8) -71

9) 132

10) 8

11) -1

12) $2a - 4$

13) $-12b + 2$

14) $-2a - 7$

15) $x^6 + 2x^4 - 5$

16) $\frac{1}{4}x^2 + 2$

Adding and Subtracting Functions.

1) -4

2) $-3a^2 + a - 3$

3) 7

4) -1

5) -6

6) $a^2 + a + 1$

7) $-x^2 - 5x - 6$

8) $-t^2 + t - 8$

9) $2u^2 + 4u + 9$

10) $-t^2 + 10t - 20$

Multiplying and Dividing Functions

1) 88

2) $3x^4 - 7x^3 + 2x^2$

3) $-35\frac{1}{2}$

4) 0

5) -19

6) $x + 1$

7) $\frac{2}{a+1}$

8) $\frac{-2a+4}{a^3 - 1}$

Composition of functions

1) -7

2) -28

3) 23

4) 19

5) -6

6) 0

7) $-10 - 2a$

8) $100 - 12a$

9) $4a^2 + 20a - 22$

10) $-x + 5 - b$

11) $-x + 3 - b$

12) $-x^2 + 5 + b$

Chapter 9:

Quadratic Functions and Matrix

Topics that you'll learn in this chapter:

- ✓ Graphing Quadratic Functions
- ✓ Solving Quadratic Equations
- ✓ Use the Quadratic Formula and the Discriminant
- ✓ Solve Quadratic Inequalities
- ✓ Adding, Subtracting and Multiplications Matrices
- ✓ Finding Determinants of a Matrix
- ✓ Finding Inverse of a Matrix
- ✓ Matrix Equations

It's fine to work on any problem, so long as it generates interesting mathematics along the way – even if you don't solve it at the end of the day." – Andrew Wiles

Graphing Quadratic Functions

✎*Sketch the graph of each function. Identify the vertex and axis of symmetry.*

1) $y = 2(x + 2)^2 - 3$

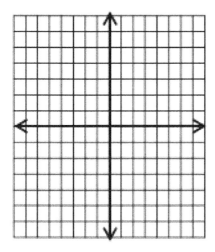

2) $y = -2(x + 2)^2 + 4$

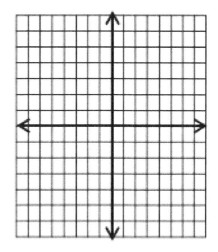

3) $x = -y^2 + 3y + 4$

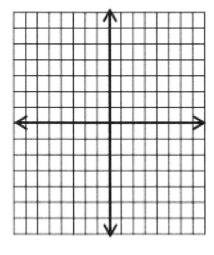

4) $y = (y + 1)^2 - 2$

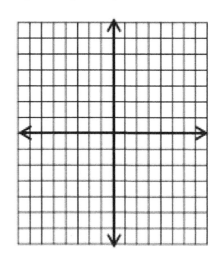

Solving Quadratic Equations

✏️ *Solve each equation by factoring or by using the quadratic formula.*

1) $x^2 + x - 20 = 2x$

2) $x^2 + 8x = -15$

3) $7x^2 - 14x = -7$

4) $6x^2 - 18x - 18 = 6$

5) $2x^2 + 6x - 24 = 12$

6) $2x^2 - 22x + 38 = -10$

7) $(2x + 5)(4x + 3) = 0$

8) $(x + 2)(x - 7) = 0$

9) $(x + 3)(x + 5) = 0$

10) $(5x + 7)(x + 4) = 0$

11) $-4x^2 - 8x - 3 = -3 - 5x^2$

12) $10x^2 = 27x - 18$

13) $7x^2 - 6x + 3 = 3$

14) $x^2 = 2x$

15) $2x^2 - 14 = -3x$

16) $10x^2 - 26x = -12$

17) $15x^2 + 80 = -80x$

18) $x^2 + 15x = -56$

Use the Quadratic Formula and the Discriminant

✎ Find the value of the discriminant of each quadratic equation.

1) $2x^2 + 5x - 4 = 0$

2) $x^2 + 5x + 2 = 0$

3) $5x^2 + x - 2 = 0$

4) $-4x^2 - 4x + 5 = 0$

5) $-2x^2 - x - 1 = 0$

6) $6x^2 - 2x - 3 = 0$

7) $x(x - 1) = 0$

8) $8x^2 - 9x = 0$

9) $3x^2 - 5x + 1 = 0$

10) $5x^2 + 6x + 4 = 0$

✎ Find the discriminant of each quadratic equation then state the number of real and imaginary solution.

11) $8x^2 - 6x + 3 = 5x^2$

12) $-4x^2 - 4x = 6$

13) $-x^2 - 9 = 6x$

14) $-9x^2 = -8x + 8$

15) $4x^2 = 8x - 4$

16) $9x^2 + 6x + 6 = 5$

17) $9x^2 - 3x - 8 = -10$

18) $-2x^2 - 8x - 14 = -6$

Solve Quadratic Inequalities

✎ **Solve each quadratic inequality.**

1) $-x^2 - 5x + 6 > 0$

2) $x^2 - 5x - 6 < 0$

3) $x^2 + 4x - 5 > 0$

4) $x^2 - 2x - 3 \geq 0$

5) $x^2 - 1 < 0$

6) $17x^2 + 15x - 2 \geq 0$

7) $4x^2 + 20x - 11 < 0$

8) $12x^2 + 10x - 12 > 0$

9) $18x^2 + 23x + 5 \leq 0$

10) $-9x^2 + 29x - 6 \geq 0$

11) $-8x^2 + 6x - 1 \leq 0$

12) $5x^2 - 15x + 10 < 0$

13) $3x^2 - 5x \geq 4x^2 + 6$

14) $x^2 > 5x + 6$

15) $3x^2 + 7x \leq 5x^2 + 3x - 6$

16) $4x^2 - 12 > 3x^2 + x$

17) $3x^2 - 5x \geq 4x^2 + 6$

18) $2x^2 + 2x - 8 > x^2$

Adding and Subtracting Matrices

✎ **Simplify.**

1) $|-6 \quad 3 \quad -4| + |2 \quad -3 \quad -1|$

2) $\begin{vmatrix} 2 & 3 \\ -1 & -2 \\ -4 & -1 \end{vmatrix} + \begin{vmatrix} 0 & -1 \\ 1 & 0 \\ 2 & 5 \end{vmatrix}$

3) $\begin{vmatrix} -2 & 0 & -1 \\ 4 & -2 & 0 \end{vmatrix} - \begin{vmatrix} 6 & -2 & -1 \\ 1 & 4 & -3 \end{vmatrix}$

4) $|5 \quad 2| + |-2 \quad -7|$

5) $\begin{vmatrix} 1 \\ 4 \end{vmatrix} + \begin{vmatrix} 3 \\ 6 \end{vmatrix}$

6) $\begin{vmatrix} -r+t \\ -r \\ 3s \end{vmatrix} + \begin{vmatrix} r \\ -2t \\ -2r+2 \end{vmatrix}$

7) $\begin{vmatrix} z-2 \\ -4 \\ -1-5z \\ 2y \end{vmatrix} + \begin{vmatrix} -y \\ z \\ 5+z \\ 4z \end{vmatrix}$

8) $\begin{vmatrix} -4n & n+m \\ -2n & -4m \end{vmatrix} + \begin{vmatrix} 4 & -2 \\ m & 0 \end{vmatrix}$

9) $\begin{vmatrix} 2 & 3 \\ -6 & 5 \end{vmatrix} - \begin{vmatrix} 0 & -3 \\ 1 & 10 \end{vmatrix}$

10) $\begin{vmatrix} 1 & -5 & 9 \\ 4 & -3 & 11 \\ -6 & 3 & -15 \end{vmatrix} + \begin{vmatrix} 3 & 4 & -5 \\ 5 & 2 & 0 \\ 4 & -5 & 1 \end{vmatrix}$

Matrix Multiplication

✎ *Simplify.*

1) $\begin{vmatrix} -1 & -1 \\ -1 & 2 \end{vmatrix} \times \begin{vmatrix} -2 & -3 \\ 3 & 2 \end{vmatrix}$

2) $\begin{vmatrix} 0 & 3 \\ -3 & 1 \\ -5 & 1 \end{vmatrix} \times \begin{vmatrix} -2 & 2 \\ -2 & -4 \end{vmatrix}$

3) $\begin{vmatrix} 4 & 2 & 5 \\ 2 & 5 & 1 \end{vmatrix} \times \begin{vmatrix} 4 & 6 & -5 \\ 5 & -1 & 0 \end{vmatrix}$

4) $\begin{vmatrix} -4 \\ 0 \\ 2 \end{vmatrix} \times \begin{vmatrix} 2 & -1 \end{vmatrix}$

5) $\begin{vmatrix} 2 & -1 \\ 0 & 6 \\ -2 & -2 \end{vmatrix} \times \begin{vmatrix} -1 & 6 \\ 5 & 4 \end{vmatrix}$

6) $\begin{vmatrix} -1 & -3 \\ -2 & 3 \\ 3 & 0 \\ 4 & -2 \end{vmatrix} \times \begin{vmatrix} 1 & -2 & 1 \\ -1 & 0 & -3 \end{vmatrix}$

7) $\begin{vmatrix} -2 & -y \\ -x & -2 \end{vmatrix} \cdot \begin{vmatrix} -x & 0 \\ y & -2 \end{vmatrix}$

8) $\begin{vmatrix} 1 & -4v \end{vmatrix} \cdot \begin{vmatrix} -2u & -v \\ 0 & 3 \end{vmatrix}$

9) $\begin{vmatrix} -1 & 1 & -1 \\ 0 & 2 & -1 \\ 2 & -5 & 1 \\ -5 & 6 & 0 \end{vmatrix} \begin{vmatrix} 2 & 1 \\ 1 & -2 \\ 3 & 0 \end{vmatrix}$

10) $\begin{vmatrix} 5 & 3 & 5 \\ 1 & 5 & 0 \end{vmatrix} \cdot \begin{vmatrix} -4 & 2 \\ -3 & 4 \\ 3 & -5 \end{vmatrix}$

11) $\begin{vmatrix} -1 & 5 \\ -2 & 1 \end{vmatrix} \cdot \begin{vmatrix} 6 & -2 \\ 1 & 0 \end{vmatrix}$

12) $\begin{vmatrix} 0 & 2 \\ -2 & -5 \end{vmatrix} \cdot \begin{vmatrix} 2 & -1 \\ 3 & 0 \end{vmatrix}$

Finding Determinants of a Matrix

✎Evaluate the determinant of each matrix.

1) $\begin{vmatrix} 0 & -3 \\ -6 & -2 \end{vmatrix}$

2) $\begin{vmatrix} 0 & 3 \\ 2 & 6 \end{vmatrix}$

3) $\begin{vmatrix} -1 & 1 \\ -1 & 2 \end{vmatrix}$

4) $\begin{vmatrix} -2 & -9 \\ -1 & -10 \end{vmatrix}$

5) $\begin{vmatrix} -1 & 6 \\ 5 & 0 \end{vmatrix}$

6) $\begin{vmatrix} 8 & -6 \\ 0 & 9 \end{vmatrix}$

7) $\begin{vmatrix} 2 & -2 \\ 5 & -4 \end{vmatrix}$

8) $\begin{vmatrix} 2 & 6 \\ 3 & 9 \end{vmatrix}$

9) $\begin{vmatrix} 0 & 2 \\ -6 & 0 \end{vmatrix}$

10) $\begin{vmatrix} 0 & 4 \\ 4 & 5 \end{vmatrix}$

11) $\begin{vmatrix} 2 & -3 & 1 \\ 2 & 0 & -1 \\ 1 & 4 & 5 \end{vmatrix}$

12) $\begin{vmatrix} -5 & 0 & -1 \\ 1 & 2 & -1 \\ -3 & 4 & 1 \end{vmatrix}$

13) $\begin{vmatrix} 6 & 1 & 1 \\ 4 & -2 & 5 \\ 2 & 8 & 7 \end{vmatrix}$

14) $\begin{vmatrix} 3 & -5 & 3 \\ 2 & 1 & -1 \\ 1 & 0 & 4 \end{vmatrix}$

15) $\begin{vmatrix} 1 & 3 & 2 \\ 3 & -1 & -3 \\ 2 & 3 & 1 \end{vmatrix}$

Finding Inverse of a Matrix

✎ *Find the inverse of each matrix.*

1) $\begin{vmatrix} 4 & 7 \\ 2 & 6 \end{vmatrix}$

8) $\begin{vmatrix} -6 & -11 \\ 2 & 7 \end{vmatrix}$

2) $\begin{vmatrix} 2 & 1 \\ 3 & 2 \end{vmatrix}$

9) $\begin{vmatrix} -1 & 8 \\ -1 & 8 \end{vmatrix}$

3) $\begin{vmatrix} 4 & 3 \\ 2 & 1 \end{vmatrix}$

10) $\begin{vmatrix} -1 & 1 \\ 6 & 3 \end{vmatrix}$

4) $\begin{vmatrix} -9 & 6 \\ 4 & 3 \end{vmatrix}$

11) $\begin{vmatrix} 11 & 5 \\ 2 & 1 \end{vmatrix}$

5) $\begin{vmatrix} -3 & 2 \\ 1 & 3 \end{vmatrix}$

12) $\begin{vmatrix} 0 & 2 \\ 1 & 9 \end{vmatrix}$

6) $\begin{vmatrix} 2 & 4 \\ 5 & 2 \end{vmatrix}$

13) $\begin{vmatrix} 0 & 0 \\ -6 & 3 \end{vmatrix}$

7) $\begin{vmatrix} 0 & 7 \\ 3 & 2 \end{vmatrix}$

14) $\begin{vmatrix} 3 & 4 \\ 6 & 8 \end{vmatrix}$

Matrix Equations

✎ *Solve each equation.*

1) $\begin{vmatrix} -1 & 2 \\ -2 & 5 \end{vmatrix} z = \begin{vmatrix} 6 \\ 20 \end{vmatrix}$

2) $2x = \begin{vmatrix} 12 & -12 \\ 24 & -8 \end{vmatrix}$

3) $\begin{vmatrix} -3 & 2 \\ -11 & 6 \end{vmatrix} = \begin{vmatrix} 2 & 8 \\ 5 & 9 \end{vmatrix} - x$

4) $Y - \begin{vmatrix} -2 \\ -4 \\ 10 \\ 10 \end{vmatrix} = \begin{vmatrix} -6 \\ 6 \\ -16 \\ 0 \end{vmatrix}$

5) $\begin{vmatrix} -1 & -3 \\ 0 & -4 \end{vmatrix} C = \begin{vmatrix} 10 \\ 8 \end{vmatrix}$

6) $\begin{vmatrix} -1 & -3 \\ 2 & 8 \end{vmatrix} B = \begin{vmatrix} -8 & -2 & 8 \\ 22 & 0 & -20 \end{vmatrix}$

7) $\begin{vmatrix} -1 & 1 \\ 5 & -2 \end{vmatrix} C = \begin{vmatrix} 1 \\ -11 \end{vmatrix}$

8) $\begin{vmatrix} 1 & 2 \\ 3 & 4 \end{vmatrix} C = \begin{vmatrix} 11 \\ 21 \end{vmatrix}$

9) $\begin{vmatrix} 0 & -4 \\ 3 & 3 \end{vmatrix} Z = \begin{vmatrix} 20 \\ 6 \end{vmatrix}$

10) $\begin{vmatrix} -10 \\ 15 \\ -20 \end{vmatrix} = 5B$

11) $\begin{vmatrix} -10 \\ 4 \\ 3 \end{vmatrix} = y - \begin{vmatrix} 7 \\ -5 \\ -11 \end{vmatrix}$

12) $-4b - \begin{vmatrix} 5 \\ 2 \\ -6 \end{vmatrix} = \begin{vmatrix} -33 \\ -2 \\ -22 \end{vmatrix}$

Answers of Worksheets – Chapter 9

Graphing quadratic functions

1)

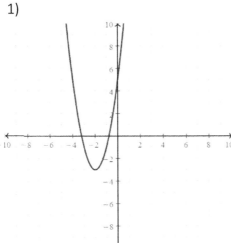

2)

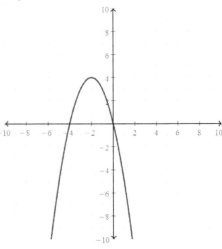

3)

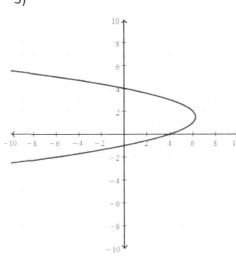

4)

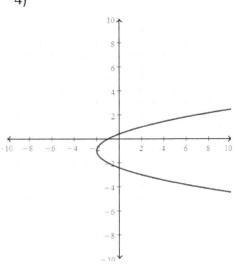

Solving quadratic equations

1) $\{5, -4\}$

2) $\{-5, -3\}$

3) $\{1\}$

4) $\{4, -1\}$

5) $\{3, -6\}$

6) $\{3, 8\}$

7) $\{-\frac{5}{2}, -\frac{3}{4}\}$

8) $\{-2, 7\}$

9) $\{-3, -5\}$

10) $\{-\frac{7}{5}, -4\}$

11) $\{8, 0\}$

12) $\{\frac{6}{5}, \frac{3}{2}\}$

15) $\{-\frac{7}{2}, 2\}$

18) $\{-8, -7\}$

13) $\{\frac{6}{7}, 0\}$

16) $\{\frac{3}{5}, 2\}$

14) $\{2, 0\}$

17) $\{-\frac{4}{3}, -4\}$

Use the quadratic formula and the discriminant

1) 57

5) −7

9) 13

2) 17

6) 76

10) −44

3) 41

7) 1

4) 96

8) 81

11) 0, one real solution

15) 0, one real solution

12) −80, no solution

16) 0, one real solution

13) 0, one real solution

17) −63, two imaginary solution

14) −224, no solution

18) 0, one real solution

Solve quadratic inequalities

1) $-6 < x < 1$

7) $-\frac{11}{2} < x < \frac{1}{2}$

12) $1 < x < 2$

2) $-1 < x < 6$

13) $-3 \le x \le -2$

8) $x < -\frac{3}{2}$ or $x > \frac{2}{3}$

3) $x < -5$ or $x > 1$

14) $x < -1$ or $x > 6$

9) $-1 \le x \le -\frac{5}{18}$

4) $x \le -1$ or $x \ge 3$

15) $x \le -1$ or $x \ge 3$

10) $\frac{2}{9} \le x \le 3$

16) $x < -3$ or $x > 4$

5) $-1 < x < 1$

17) $-3 \le x \le -2$

6) $x \le -1$ or $x \ge \frac{2}{17}$

11) $x \le \frac{1}{4}$ or $x \ge \frac{1}{2}$

18) $x < -4$ or $x > 2$

Adding and Subtracting Matrices

1) $\begin{vmatrix} -4 & 0 & -5 \end{vmatrix}$

3) $\begin{vmatrix} -8 & 2 & 0 \\ 3 & -6 & 3 \end{vmatrix}$

2) $\begin{vmatrix} 2 & 2 \\ 0 & -2 \\ -2 & 4 \end{vmatrix}$

4) $\begin{vmatrix} 3 & -5 \end{vmatrix}$

5) $\begin{vmatrix} 4 \\ 10 \end{vmatrix}$

6) $\begin{vmatrix} t \\ -r-2t \\ 3s-2r+2 \end{vmatrix}$

7) $\begin{vmatrix} z-2-y \\ -4+z \\ 4-4z \\ 2y+4z \end{vmatrix}$

8) $\begin{vmatrix} -4n+4 & n+m-2 \\ -2n+m & -4m \end{vmatrix}$

9) $\begin{vmatrix} 2 & 6 \\ -7 & -5 \end{vmatrix}$

10) $\begin{vmatrix} 4 & -1 & 4 \\ 9 & -1 & 11 \\ -2 & -2 & -14 \end{vmatrix}$

Matrix Multiplication

1) $\begin{vmatrix} -1 & 1 \\ 8 & 7 \end{vmatrix}$

2) $\begin{vmatrix} -6 & -12 \\ 4 & -10 \\ 8 & -14 \end{vmatrix}$

3) Undefined

4) $\begin{vmatrix} -8 & 4 \\ 0 & 0 \\ 4 & -2 \end{vmatrix}$

5) $\begin{vmatrix} -7 & 8 \\ 30 & 24 \\ -8 & -20 \end{vmatrix}$

6) $\begin{vmatrix} 2 & 2 & 8 \\ -5 & 4 & -11 \\ 3 & -6 & 3 \\ 6 & -8 & 10 \end{vmatrix}$

7) $\begin{vmatrix} 2x-y^2 & 0 \\ x^2-2y & 4 \end{vmatrix}$

8) $\begin{vmatrix} -2u & -13v \end{vmatrix}$

9) $\begin{vmatrix} -4 & -3 \\ -1 & -4 \\ 2 & 12 \\ -4 & -17 \end{vmatrix}$

10) $\begin{vmatrix} -14 & -3 \\ -19 & 22 \end{vmatrix}$

11) $\begin{vmatrix} -1 & 2 \\ -11 & 4 \end{vmatrix}$

12) $\begin{vmatrix} 6 & 0 \\ -19 & 2 \end{vmatrix}$

Finding Determinants of a Matrix

1) −18

2) -6

3) −1

4) 11

5) −30

6) 72

7) 2

8) 0

9) 12

10) −16

11) 49

12) -40

13) −30

14) 54

15) 3

Finding Inverse of a Matrix

1) $\begin{vmatrix} \dfrac{6}{10} & \dfrac{-7}{10} \\ \dfrac{-1}{5} & \dfrac{2}{5} \end{vmatrix}$

2) $\begin{vmatrix} 2 & -1 \\ -3 & 2 \end{vmatrix}$

3) $\begin{vmatrix} -\dfrac{1}{2} & \dfrac{3}{2} \\ 1 & -2 \end{vmatrix}$

4) $\begin{vmatrix} -\dfrac{3}{51} & \dfrac{6}{51} \\ \dfrac{4}{51} & \dfrac{9}{51} \end{vmatrix}$

5) $\begin{vmatrix} -\dfrac{3}{11} & \dfrac{2}{11} \\ \dfrac{1}{11} & \dfrac{3}{11} \end{vmatrix}$

6) $\begin{vmatrix} -\dfrac{2}{16} & \dfrac{4}{16} \\ \dfrac{5}{16} & -\dfrac{2}{16} \end{vmatrix}$

7) $\begin{vmatrix} -\dfrac{2}{21} & \dfrac{7}{21} \\ \dfrac{3}{21} & 0 \end{vmatrix}$

8) $\begin{vmatrix} -\dfrac{7}{20} & -\dfrac{11}{20} \\ \dfrac{2}{20} & \dfrac{6}{20} \end{vmatrix}$

9) No inverse exists

10) $\begin{vmatrix} -\dfrac{3}{9} & \dfrac{1}{9} \\ \dfrac{6}{9} & \dfrac{1}{9} \end{vmatrix}$

11) $\begin{vmatrix} 1 & -5 \\ -2 & 11 \end{vmatrix}$

12) $\begin{vmatrix} -\dfrac{9}{2} & 1 \\ \dfrac{1}{2} & 0 \end{vmatrix}$

13) No inverse exists

14) No inverse exists

Matrix Equations

1) $\begin{vmatrix} 10 \\ 8 \end{vmatrix}$

2) $\begin{vmatrix} 6 & -6 \\ 12 & -4 \end{vmatrix}$

3) $\begin{vmatrix} 5 & 6 \\ 16 & 3 \end{vmatrix}$

4) $\begin{vmatrix} -4 \\ 2 \\ -6 \\ 10 \end{vmatrix}$

5) $\begin{vmatrix} -4 \\ -2 \end{vmatrix}$

6) $\begin{vmatrix} -1 & 8 & -2 \\ 3 & -2 & -2 \end{vmatrix}$

7) $\begin{vmatrix} -3 \\ -2 \end{vmatrix}$

8) $\begin{vmatrix} -1 \\ 6 \end{vmatrix}$

9) $\begin{vmatrix} 7 \\ -5 \end{vmatrix}$

10) $\begin{vmatrix} -2 \\ 3 \\ -4 \end{vmatrix}$

11) $\begin{vmatrix} -3 \\ -1 \\ -8 \end{vmatrix}$

12) $\begin{vmatrix} 7 \\ 0 \\ 7 \end{vmatrix}$

Chapter 10: Logarithms

Topics that you'll learn in this chapter:

✓ Rewriting Logarithms

✓ Evaluating Logarithms

✓ Properties of Logarithms

✓ Natural Logarithms

✓ Solving Exponential Equations Requiring Logarithms

✓ Solving Logarithmic Equations

Mathematics is an art of human understanding. — William Thurston

Rewriting Logarithms

Rewrite each equation in exponential form.

1) $\log_{0.81} 0.9 = \frac{1}{2}$

3) $\log_8 64 = 2$

2) $\log_{100} 1000 = 1.50$

4) $\log_{10} 100 = 2$

Rewrite each equation in exponential form.

5) $\log_a \frac{6}{7} = b$

8) $\log_y x = -9$

6) $\log_x y = 8$

9) $\log_a b = 33$

7) $\log_{15} n = m$

10) $\log_{\frac{1}{3}} v = u$

Evaluate each expression.

11) $\log_3 27$

13) $\log_5 25$

12) $\log_6 216$

14) $\log_8 4$

Evaluating Logarithms

Evaluate each expression.

1) $\log_2 16$

8) $\log_{80} 300$

2) $\log_3 81$

9) $\log_5 \frac{1}{125}$

3) $\log_2 8$

10) $\log_4 256$

4) $\log_3 9$

11) $\log_7 343$

5) $\log_9 81$

12) $\log_3 \frac{1}{27}$

6) $\log_6 \frac{1}{36}$

13) $\log_9 729$

7) $\log_{27} \frac{1}{3}$

14) $\log_8 4096$

Properties of Logarithms

✑Expand each logarithm.

1) $\log \left(\frac{4}{5}\right)^3$

2) $\log (7.3^3)$

3) $\log \left(\frac{5}{7}\right)^2$

4) $\log \frac{3^3}{5}$

5) $\log (x . y)^7$

6) $\log (3 . 8)$

7) $\log (2 . 5)$

8) $\log (x^4 . y . z^5)$

9) $\log \frac{u^3}{v}$

10) $\log \frac{x}{y^9}$

✑Condense each expression to a single logarithm.

11) $log\ 4 - \log 7$

12) $4 \log 3 - 3 \log 2$

13) $\log 5 - 3 \log 11$

14) $5 \log_7 a + 9 \log_7 b$

15) $2\log_2 x - 5 \log_2 y$

16) $\log_6 u - 7 \log_6 v$

17) $2 \log_6 u + 5 \log_6 v$

18) $6 \log_5 u - 10 \log_5 v$

Natural Logarithms

✑Solve.

1) $e^x = 2$

2) $\ln (\ln x) = 7$

3) $e^x = 6$

4) $\ln (5x + 6) = 4$

5) $\ln (9x - 1) = 1$

6) $\ln x = \frac{1}{3}$

7) $x = e^{\frac{1}{2}}$

8) $\ln x = \ln 3 + \ln 8$

✎ *Evaluate without using a calculator.*

9) $\ln\sqrt{e}$

13) $e^{\ln 12}$

10) $\ln e^5$

14) $e^{3\ln 3}$

11) $6 \ln e$

15) $e^{4\ln 2}$

12) $\ln\left(\frac{1}{e}\right)$

16) $\ln 1$

Solving Exponential Equations Requiring Logarithms

✎ *Solve each equation.*

1) $2^{r+1} = 1$

10) $2^{-2x} = 2^{x-1}$

2) $216^x = 36$

11) $2^{2n} = 64$

3) $4^{-3v-3} = 16$

12) $6^{3n} = 216$

4) $4^{2n} = 16$

13) $4^{-2k} = 256$

5) $\frac{216^{2a}}{36^{-a}} = 216$

14) $6^{2r} = 6^{3r}$

6) $24.\ 24^{-v} = 576$

15) $10^{5x} = 10000$

7) $2^{2n} = 4$

16) $36.\ 6^{-v} = 216$

8) $\left(\frac{1}{7}\right)^n = 49$

17) $\frac{64}{16^{-3m}} = 16^{-2m-2}$

9) $32^{2x} = 4$

18) $3^{-2n}.\ 3^{n+1} = 3^{-2n}$

Solving Logarithmic Equations

✎ *Solve each equation.*

1) $2 \log_6 - 2x = 0$

2) $- \log_2 3x = 2$

3) $\log x + 6 = 3$

4) $\log x - \log 2 = 1$

5) $\log x + \log 2 = 2$

6) $\log 5 + \log x = 1$

7) $\log x + \log 8 = \log 16$

8) $- 2 \log_2 (x - 3) = - 10$

9) $\log 7x = \log (x + 6)$

10) $\log(9k - 5) = \log(3k - 1)$

11) $\log(5p - 1) = \log(- 4p + 6)$

12) $- 10 + \log_3 (n + 2) = - 10$

13) $\log_8 (12x + 3) = \log_8 (x^2 + 30)$

14) $\log_{12} (v^2 - 38) = \log_{12} (- 5v - 2)$

15) $\log(12 + 2b) = \log(b^2 - 2b)$

16) $\log_8 (x + 4) - \log_8 x = \log_8 2$

17) $\log_2 4 + \log_2 x^2 = \log_2 36$

18) $\log_8 (x + 1) - \log_8 x = \log_8 32$

Answers of Worksheets – Chapter 10

Rewriting Logarithms

1) $0.81^{\frac{1}{2}} = 0.9$

2) $100^{1.5} = 1000$

3) $8^2 = 64$

4) $10^2 = 100$

5) $a^b = \frac{6}{7}$

6) $x^8 = y$

7) $15^m = n$

8) $y^{-9} = x$

9) $a^{33} = b$

10) $(\frac{1}{3})^u = v$

11) 3

12) 3

13) 2

14) $\frac{2}{3}$

Evaluating Logarithms

1) 4

2) 4

3) 3

4) 2

5) 2

6) -2

7) $-\frac{1}{3}$

8) 1.3

9) -3

10) 4

11) 3

12) -3

13) 3

14) 4

Properties of Logarithms

1) $3 \log 4 - 3 \log 5$

2) $\log 7 + 3 \log 3$

3) $2\log 5 - 2 \log 7$

4) $3 \log 3 - \log 5$

5) $7 \log x + 7 \log y$

6) $\log 3 + \log 8$

7) $\log 2 + \log 5$

8) $4\log x + \log y + 5 \log z$

9) $3 \log u - \log v$

10) $\log x - 9 \log y$

11) $\log \frac{4}{7}$

12) $\log \frac{3^4}{2^3}$

13) $\log \frac{5}{11^3}$

14) $\log_7 (a^5 b^9)$

15) $\log_2 \frac{x^2}{y^5}$

16) $\log_6 \frac{u}{v^7}$

17) $\log_6 (v^5 u^2)$

18) $\log_5 \frac{u^6}{v^{10}}$

Natural Logarithms

1) $x = \ln 2$

2) $x = e^{e^7}$

3) $x = \ln 6$

4) $x = \dfrac{e^4 - 6}{5}$

5) $x = \dfrac{e + 1}{9}$

6) $x = e^{\frac{1}{3}}$

7) $\ln x = \dfrac{1}{2}$

8) $x = 24$

9) $\dfrac{1}{2}$

10) 5

11) 6

12) −1

13) 12

14) 27

15) 16

16) 0

Solving Exponential Equations Requiring Logarithms

1) − 1

2) $\dfrac{1}{12}$

3) $-\dfrac{5}{3}$

4) 1

5) $\{\frac{3}{8}\}$

6) −1

7) 1

8) −2

9) $\dfrac{1}{5}$

10) $\dfrac{1}{3}$

11) 3

12) 1

13) −2

14) 0

15) $\dfrac{4}{5}$

16) − 1

17) $-\dfrac{7}{10}$

18) −1

Solving Logarithmic Equations

1) $\{-\frac{1}{2}\}$

2) {12}

3) $\{\frac{1}{1000}\}$

4) {20}

5) {50}

6) {2}

7) {2}

8) {35}

9) {1}

10) $\{\frac{2}{3}\}$

11) $\{\frac{7}{9}\}$

12) {−1}

13) {9, 3}

14) {−9, 4}

15) {6, −2}

16) {4}

17) {3, −3}

18) $\{\frac{1}{31}\}$

Chapter 11: Geometry

Topics that you'll learn in this chapter:

✓ The Pythagorean Theorem

✓ Area of Triangles and Trapezoids

✓ Area and Circumference of Circles

✓ Area and Perimeter of Polygons

✓ Area of Squares, Rectangles, and Parallelograms

✓ Volume of Cubes, Rectangle Prisms, and Cylinder

✓ Surface Area of Cubes, Rectangle Prisms, and Cylinder

Mathematics is, as it were, a sensuous logic, and relates to philosophy as do the arts, music, and plastic art to poetry. — *K. Shegel*

The Pythagorean Theorem

✍ Do the following lengths form a right triangle?

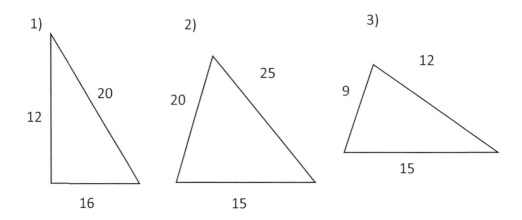

1) 20 12 16

2) 25 20 15

3) 12 9 15

✍ *Find each missing length to the nearest tenth.*

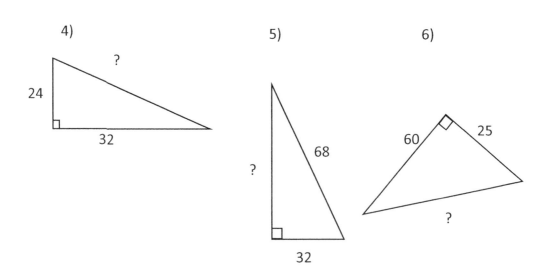

4) ? 24 32

5) 68 ? 32

6) 60 25 ?

Angles

✎ **What is the value of x in the following figures?**

1)

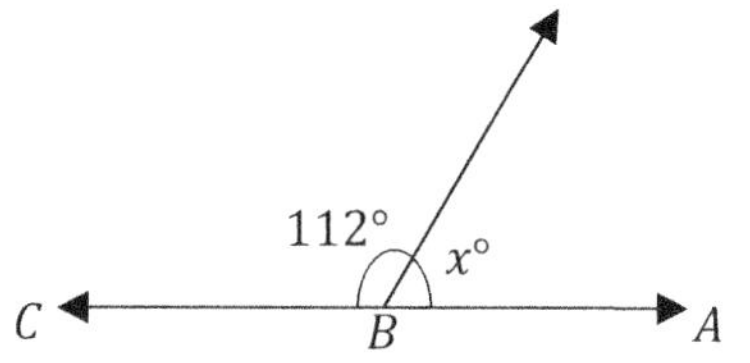

$112°$ $x°$
C ◄———— B ————► A

2)

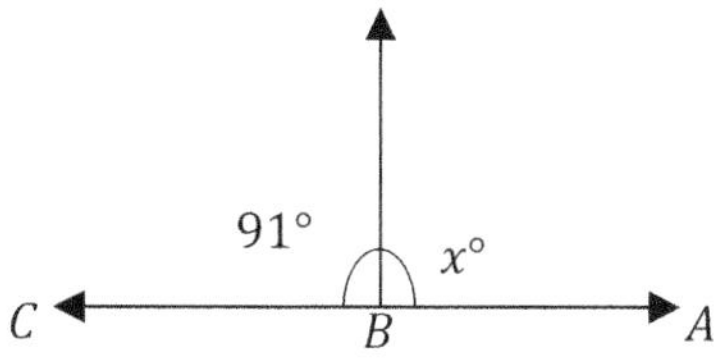

$91°$ $x°$
C ◄———— B ————► A

3)

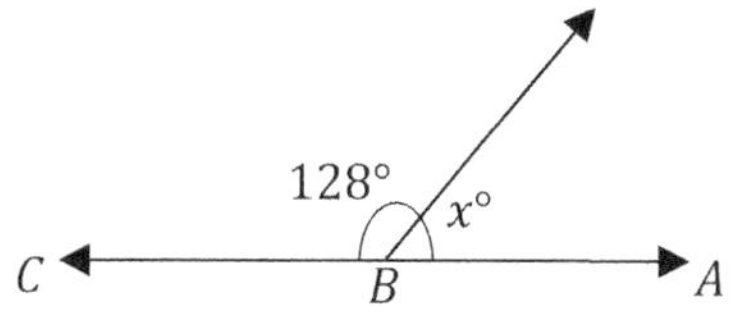

$128°$ $x°$
C ◄———— B ————► A

4)

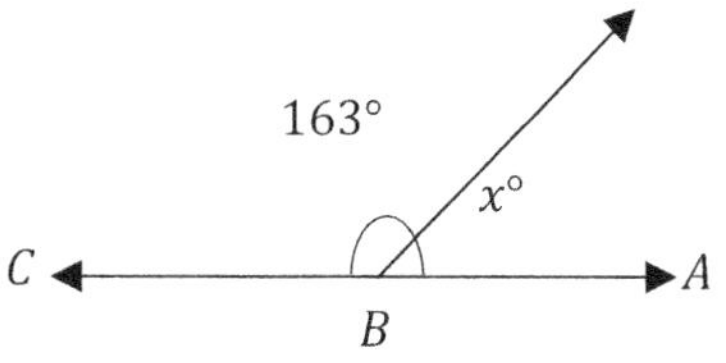

$163°$ $x°$
C ◄———— B ————► A

5)

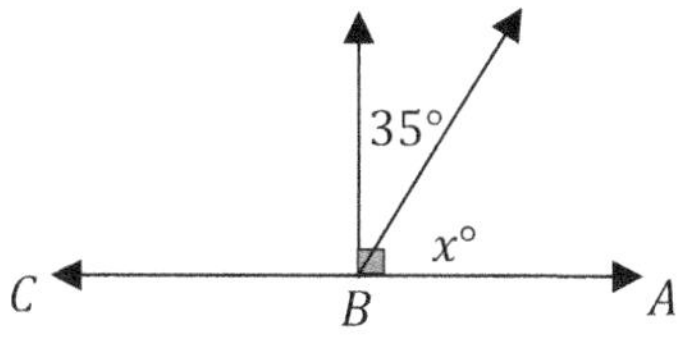

$35°$ $x°$
C ◄———— B ————► A

6)

$62°$ $x°$
C ◄———— B ————► A

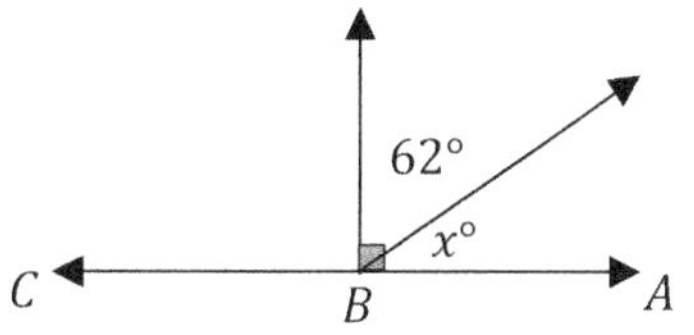

✎ *Solve.*

7) Two complementary angles have equal measures. What is the measure of each angle? _____

8) The measure of an angle is two third the measure of its supplement.What is the measure of the angle? _____

Area of Triangles

✎ **Find the area of each.**

1)

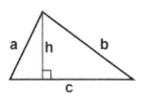

c = 12 mi

h = 4.5 mi

2)

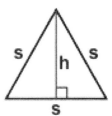

s = 8 m

h = 9.4 m

3)

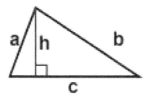

a = 4 m

b = 11 m

c = 16 m

h = 13.6 m

4)

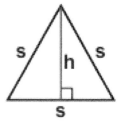

s = 6 m

h = 6.71 m

Area of Trapezoids

Calculate the area for each trapezoid.

1)

11 cm

7 cm

13 cm

2)

18 m

12 m

24 m

3)

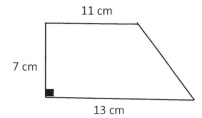

5 mi

14 mi

17 mi

5 mi

4)

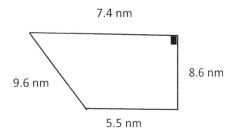

7.4 nm

9.6 nm

8.6 nm

5.5 nm

Area and Perimeter of Polygons

✍ **Find the area and perimeter of each**

1)

18 yd

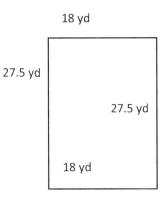

27.5 yd

27.5 yd

18 yd

2)

21mi

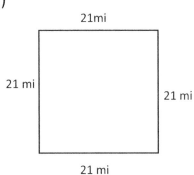

21 mi

21 mi

21 mi

3)

15.2 ft

12.8 ft

10 ft

12.8 ft

15.2 ft

4)

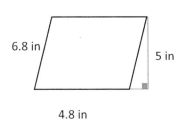

6.8 in

5 in

4.8 in

5)

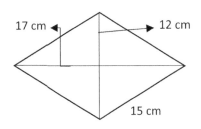

17 cm

12 cm

15 cm

6)

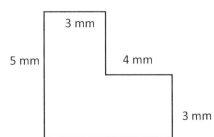

3 mm

5 mm

4 mm

3 mm

✎ **Find the perimeter of each shape.**

7)

7 m

7 m   7 m

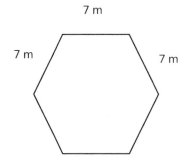

8)

12 mm

12 mm

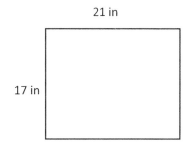

9)

16 ft   16 ft

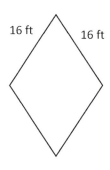

10)

21 in

17 in

11)

14 cm

12)

5.1 ft

12.4 ft

6.2 ft

17.1 ft

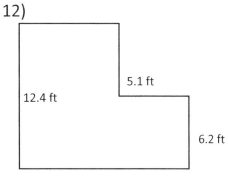

Area and Circumference of Circles

✎ **Find the area and circumference of each.** ($\pi = 3.14$)

1)

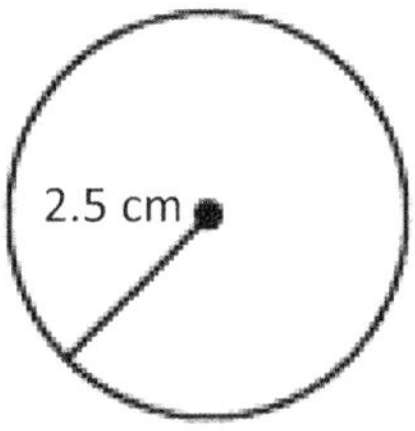

2.5 cm

2)

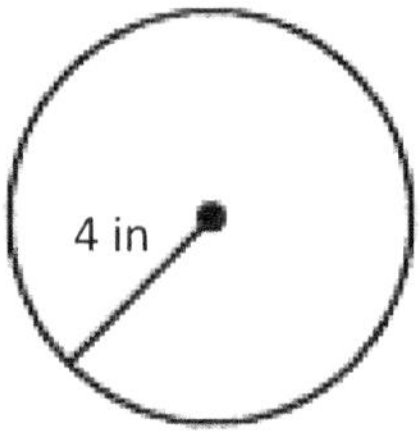

4 in

3)

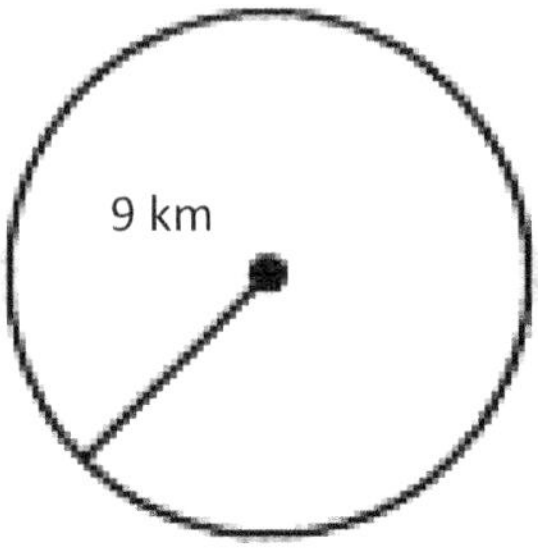

9 km

4)

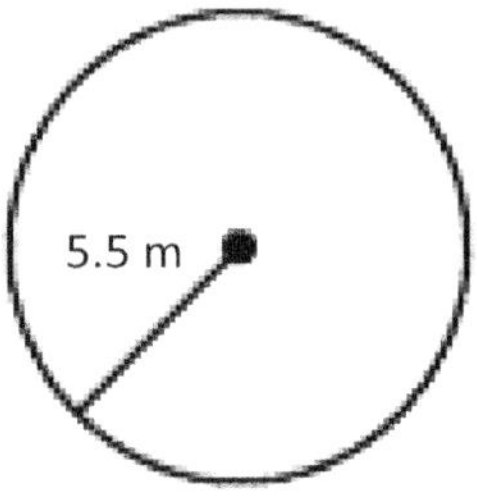

5.5 m

5)

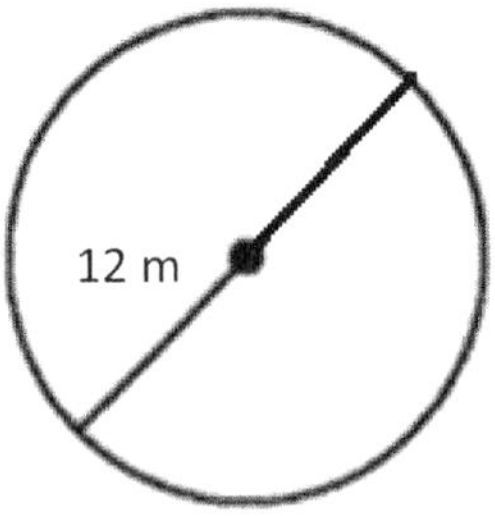

12 m

6)

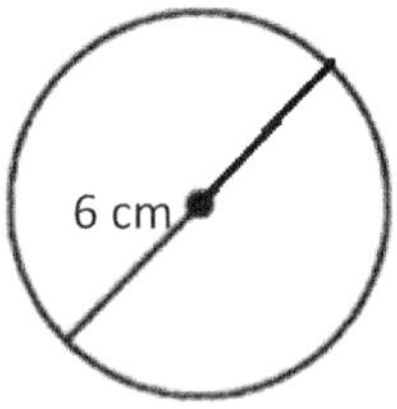

6 cm

7)

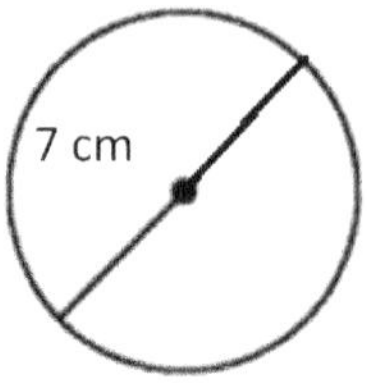

7 cm

8)

3 in

Volume of Cubes

✎ **Find the volume of each.**

1)

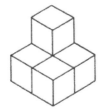

2)

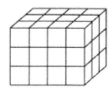

3)

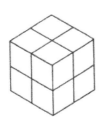

4)

5)

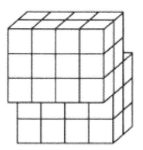

6)

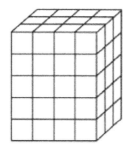

Volume of Rectangle Prisms

✎ **Find the volume of each of the rectangular prisms.**

1)

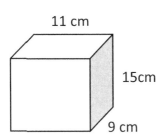
11 cm · 15cm · 9 cm

2)

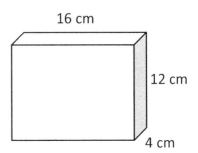
16 cm · 12 cm · 4 cm

3)

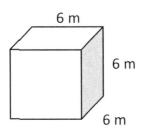
6 m · 6 m · 6 m

4)

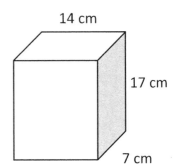
14 cm · 17 cm · 7 cm

5)

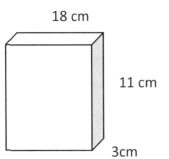
18 cm · 11 cm · 3cm

6)

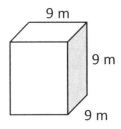
9 m · 9 m · 9 m

Surface Area of Cubes

✏️ **Find the surface of each cube.**

1)

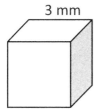

3 mm

2)

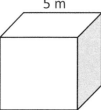

11 mm

3)

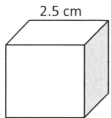

2.5 cm

4)

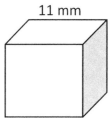

5 m

5)

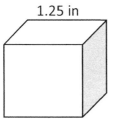

1.25 in

6)

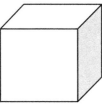

4.2 ft

Surface Area of a Rectangle Prism

✎ **Find the surface of each prism.**

1)

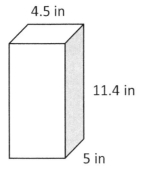

4 yd
5 yd
8 yd

2)

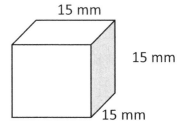

15 mm
15 mm
15 mm

3)

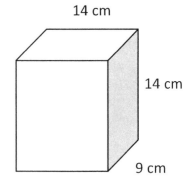

4.5 in
11.4 in
5 in

4)

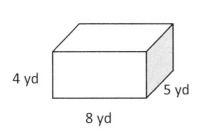

14 cm
14 cm
9 cm

Volume of a Cylinder

✎ **Find the volume of each cylinder.** ($\pi = 3.14$)

1)

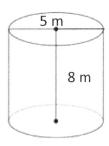

2)

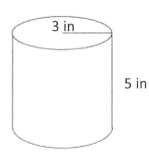

3)

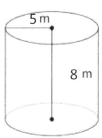

4)

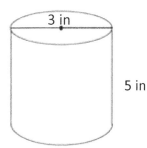

5)

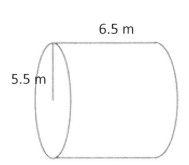

6)

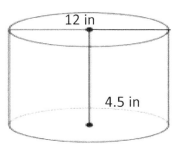

Surface Area of a Cylinder

Find the surface of each cylinder. ($\pi = 3.14$)

1)

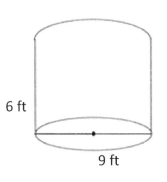

6 ft

9 ft

2)

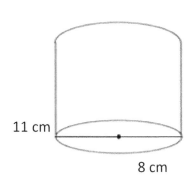

11 cm

8 cm

3)

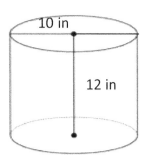

10 in

12 in

4)

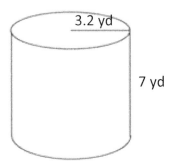

3.2 yd

7 yd

5)

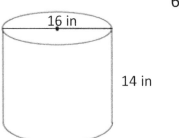

16 in

14 in

6)

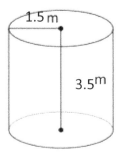

1.5 m

3.5 m

Answers of Worksheets – Chapter 11

The Pythagorean Theorem

1) yes

2) yes

3) yes

4) 40

5) 60

6) 65

Angles

1) 68°

2) 89°

3) 52°

4) 17°

5) 55°

6) 28°

7) 45°

8) 72°

Area of Triangles

1) 27 mi^2

2) 37.6 m^2

3) 108.8 m^2

4) 20.13 m^2

Area of Trapezoids

1) 84 cm^2

2) 252 m^2

3) 62 mi^2

4) 55.47 nm^2

Area of Squares, Rectangles, and Parallelograms

1) Area: 495 m^2, P: 91

2) Area: 441 mm^2, Perimeter: 84

3) Area: 128 ft^2, Perimeter: 56 ft

4) Area: 24 in^2, Perimeter: 23.2in

5) Area: 102 cm^2, Perimeter 60 cm

6) Area: 27 mm^2, Perimeter:24 mi

7) P: 42 m

8) P: 48 mm

9) P: 64 ft

10) P: 76 in

11) P: 56 cm

12) P: 59 ft

Area and Circumference of Circles

1) Area: 19.63 cm^2, Circumference: 15.7 cm.

2) Area: 50.24 in^2, Circumference: 25.12 in.

3) Area: 254.34 km^2, Circumference: 56.52 km.

4) Area: 94.99 m^2, Circumference: 34.54 m.

5) Area: 113.04 m^2, Circumference: 37.68 m

6) Area: 28.26 cm^2, Circumference: 18.84 cm.

7) Area: 38.47 cm^2, Circumference: 21.98 cm.

8) Area: 7.07 in^2, Circumference: 9.42 in.

Volumes of Cubes

1) 5	3) 8	5) 44
2) 36	4) 4	6) 60

Volume of Rectangle Prisms

1) 1485 cm^3	3) 216 m^3	5) 594 cm^3
2) 768 cm^3	4) 1666 cm^3	6) 729 cm^3

Surface Area of a Cube

1) 54 mm^2	3) 37.5 cm^2	5) 9.375 in^2
2) 726 mm^2	4) 150 m^2	6) 105.84 ft^2

Surface Area of a Rectangle Prism

1) 184 yd^2	3) 261.6 in^2
2) 1350 mm^2	4) 896 cm^2

Volume of a Cylinder

1) 141.3 cm^3	3) 157 m^3	5) 617.4 m^3
2) 628 cm^3	4) 35.325 m^3	6) 508.68 m^3

Surface Area of a Cylinder

1) 296.73 ft^2	3) 533.8 in^2	5) 1105.28 in^2
2) 376.8 cm^2	4) 204.98 yd^2	6) 47.1m^2

Chapter 12: Sequences and Series

Topics that you'll learn in this chapter:

- ✓ Arithmetic Sequences
- ✓ Geometric Sequences
- ✓ Comparing Arithmetic and Geometric Sequences
- ✓ Finite Geometric Series
- ✓ Infinite Geometric Series

Mathematics is like checkers in being suitable for the young, not too difficult, amusing, and without peril to the state. – Plato

Arithmetic Sequences

✎Given the first term and the common difference of an arithmetic sequence find the first five terms and the explicit formula.

1) $a_1 = 23, d = 2$

3) $a_1 = 15, d = 10$

2) $a_1 = -10, d = -2$

4) $a_1 = -30, d = -50$

✎Given a term in an arithmetic sequence and the common difference find the first five terms and the explicit formula.

5) $a_{36} = -248, d = -6$

7) $a_{38} = -52.3, d = -1.1$

6) $a_{34} = 156, d = 5$

8) $a_{20} = -591, d = -30$

✎Given a term in an arithmetic sequence and the common difference find the recursive formula and the three terms in the sequence after the last one given.

9) $a_{22} = -46, d = -2$

11) $a_{18} = 26.4, d = 1.1$

10) $a_{12} = 28.6, d = 1.2$

12) $a_{32} = -1.2, d = 0.6$

Geometric Sequences

✏️ Determine if the sequence is geometric. If it is, find the common ratio.

1) -1, 5, -25, 125, …

3) 3, 16, 23, 64, …

2) $-3, -9, -27, -81, \ldots$

4) $-2, -8, -16, -32, \ldots$

✏️ Given the first term and the common ratio of a geometric sequence find the first five terms and the explicit formula.

5) $a_1 = 0.6, r = -5$

6) $a_1 = 1, r = 3$

✏️ Given the recursive formula for a geometric sequence find the common ratio, the first five terms, and the explicit formula.

7) $a_n = a_{n-1}. 2, a_1 = 3$

9) $a_n = a_{n-1}. 5, a_1 = 1$

8) $a_n = a_{n-1}. -2, a_1 = -2$

10) $a_n = a_{n-1} . \frac{1}{3}, a_1 = -3$

✏️ Given two terms in a geometric sequence find the 8th term and the recursive formula.

11) $a_4 = 216$ and $a_5 = -1296$

12) $a_5 = -32$ and $a_2 = -4$

Comparing Arithmetic and Geometric Sequences

✍ **For each sequence, state if it arithmetic, geometric, or neither.**

1) 1, 3, 6, 9, 12, …

2) 1, 4, 16, 64, 256, …

3) 4, 24, 64, 100, …

4) −28, −30, −32, −34, −36, …

5) −5, 15, −45, 135, −405, …

6) 40, 43, 46, 49, 52, …

7) 1, 4, 7, 10, 13, …

8) −34, −27, −20, −13, −6, …

9) $a_n = -145 + 200_n$

10) $a_n = 16 + 3_n$

11) $a_n = -2 \cdot (-3)^{n-1}$

12) $a_n = -23 + 4_n$

13) $a_n = (3n)^2$

14) $a_n = -40 + 7_n$

15) $a_n = -(-2)^{n-1}$

16) $a_n = 3 \cdot (-3)^{n-1}$

Finite Geometric Series

✎ **Evaluate the related series of each sequence.**

1) $1, -6, 36, -216$

3) $7, -21, 61, -183$

2) $4, 8, 16, 32, 64$

4) $-2, 1, -\frac{1}{2}, \frac{1}{4}, -\frac{1}{8}$

✎ **Evaluate each geometric series described.**

5) $1 + 5 + 25 + 125 \ldots, n = 6$

13) $\sum_{p=1}^{6} (-3) \cdot (-4)^{p-1}$

6) $1 - 3 + 9 - 27 \ldots, n = 9$

14) $\sum_{m=1}^{9} (-3)^{m-1} 6$

7) $-2 - 8 - 32 - 128 \ldots, n = 9$

15) $\sum_{n=1}^{9} 3^{n-1} 6$

8) $4 - 8 + 16 - 32 \ldots, n = 7$

9) $1 + \frac{1}{2} + \frac{1}{4} + \frac{1}{8} \ldots, n = 6$

16) $\sum_{n=1}^{4} (\frac{1}{3})^{n-1} 4$

10) $-5 - 5 - 5 - 5 \ldots, n = 12$

17) $\sum_{n=1}^{6} 4^{n-1} + \sum_{j=1}^{7} (-3)^{j-1}$

11) $\sum_{n=1}^{8} 2 \cdot (-3)^{n-1}$

18) $5 \sum_{n=1}^{8} 5^{n-1}$

12) $\sum_{n=1}^{10} 5 \cdot 2^{n-1}$

Infinite Geometric Series

✎ **Determine if each geometric series converges or diverges.**

1) $a_1 = -1, r = 3$

2) $a_1 = -3, r = 4$

3) $a_1 = 5.5, r = 0.5$

4) $81 + 27 + 9 + 3 \ldots,$

5) $-3 + \dfrac{12}{5} - \dfrac{48}{25} + \dfrac{192}{125} \ldots,$

6) $\dfrac{128}{3125} - \dfrac{64}{625} + \dfrac{32}{125} - \dfrac{16}{25} \ldots,$

✎ **Evaluate each infinite geometric series described.**

7) $a_1 = 3, r = -\dfrac{1}{5}$

8) $a_1 = 1, r = -4$

9) $a_1 = 1, r = -3$

10) $a_1 = 3, r = \dfrac{1}{2}$

11) $1 + 0.5 + 0.25 + 0.125 + \ldots$

12) $1 - 0.6 + 0.36 - 0.216 \ldots,$

13) $81 - 27 + 9 - 3 \ldots,$

14) $3 + \dfrac{9}{4} + \dfrac{27}{16} + \dfrac{81}{64} \ldots,$

15) $\sum_{k=1}^{\infty} 4^{k-1}$

16) $\sum_{i=1}^{\infty} \left(\dfrac{1}{3}\right)^{i-1}$

Answers of Worksheets – Chapter 12

Arithmetic Sequences

1) First Five Terms: 23, 25, 27, 29, 31, Explicit: $a_n = 23 + 2(n-1)$

2) First Five Terms: −10, −12, −14, −16, −18, Explicit: $a_n = -10 - 2(n-1)$

3) First Five Terms: 15, 25, 35, 45, 55, Explicit: $a_n = 15 + 10(n-1)$

4) First Five Terms: −30, −80, −130, −180, −230,

   Explicit: $a_n = -30 - 50(n-1)$

5) First Five Terms: −38, −44, −50, −56, −62, Explicit: $a_n = -38 - 6(n-1)$

6) First Five Terms: −9, −4, 1, 6, 11, Explicit: $a_n = -9 + 5(n-1)$

7) First Five Terms: −11.6, −12.7, −13.8, −14.9, −16,

   Explicit: $a_n = -11.6 - 1.1(n-1)$

8) First Five Terms: −21, −51, −81, −111, −141,

   Explicit: $a_n = -21 - 30(n-1)$

9) Next 3 terms: −48, −50, −52, Recursive: $a_n = a_{n-1} - 2$, $a_1 = -4$

10) Next 3 terms: 29.8, 31, 32.2, Recursive: $a_n = a_{n-1} + 1.2$, $a_1 = 15.4$

11) Next 3 terms: 27.5, 28.6, 29.7, Recursive: $a_n = a_{n-1} + 1.1$, $a_1 = 7.7$

12) Next 3 terms: −0.6, 0, 0.6, Recursive: $a_n = a_{n-1} + 0.6$, $a_1 = -19.8$

Geometric Sequences

1) $r = -5$ 2) $r = 3$ 3) not geometric 4) not geometric

5) First Five Terms: 0.6, −3, 15, −75, 375; Explicit: $a_n = 0.6 \cdot (-5)^{n-1}$

6) First Five Terms: 1, 3, 9, 27, 81; Explicit: $a_n = 3^{n-1}$

7) Common Ratio: $r = 2$; First Five Terms: 3, 6, 12, 24. 48

   Explicit: $a_n = 3 \cdot 2^{n-1}$

8) Common Ratio: $r = -2$; First Five Terms: −2, 4, −8, 16, −32

   Explicit: $a_n = -2 \cdot (-2)^{n-1}$

9) Common Ratio: $r = 5$; First Five Terms: 1, 5, 25, 125, 625

Explicit: $a_n = 1.5^{n-1}$

10) Common Ratio: r = 2; First Five Terms: $-3, -1, -\frac{1}{3}, -\frac{1}{9}, -\frac{1}{27}$

Explicit: $an = -3.\left(\frac{1}{3}\right)^{n-1}$

11) $a_8 = -279936$, Recursive: $a_n = a_{n-1}.-6$, $a_1 = 1$

12) $a_8 = -256$, Recursive: $a_n = a_{n-1}.2$, $a_1 = -2$

Comparing Arithmetic and Geometric Sequences

1) Neither

2) Geometric

3) Neither

4) Arithmetic

5) Geometric

6) Arithmetic

7) Neither

8) Arithmetic

9) Arithmetic

10) Arithmetic

11) Geometric

12) Arithmetic

13) Neither

14) Arithmetic

15) Geometric

16) Geometric

Finite Geometric

1) -185

2) 124

3) -140

4) $-\frac{11}{8}$

5) 3,906

6) 4,921

7) $-174,762$

8) 172

9) $\frac{63}{32}$

10) -60

11) $-3,280$

12) 5,115

13) 2,457

14) 29,526

15) 59,046

16) $\frac{160}{27}$

17) 1,912

18) 488,280

Infinite Geometric

1) Diverges

2) Diverges

3) Converges

4) Converges

5) Converges

6) Diverges

7) $\frac{5}{2}$

8) No sum

9) No sum

10) 6

11) 2

12) 0.625

13) $\frac{243}{4}$

14) 12

15) No sum

16) $\frac{3}{2}$

Chapter 13: Trigonometric Functions

Topics that you'll learn in this chapter:

- ✓ Trig ratios of General Angles
- ✓ Sketch Each Angle in Standard Position
- ✓ Finding Co–Terminal Angles and Reference Angles
- ✓ Writing Each Measure in Radians
- ✓ Writing Each Measure in Degrees
- ✓ Evaluating Each Trigonometric Expression
- ✓ Missing Sides and Angles of a Right Triangle
- ✓ Arc Length and Sector Area

Mathematics is like checkers in being suitable for the young, not too difficult, amusing, and without peril to the state. – Plato

Trig ratios of General Angles

Use a calculator to find each. Round your answers to the

nearest ten–thousandth.

1) $\sin - 150°$

4) $\cos 120°$

2) $\sin 120°$

5) $\sin 180°$

3) $\cos 315°$

6) $\sin - 300°$

Find the exact value of each trigonometric function.

Some may be undefined.

7) $\sec -120$

8) $\tan -\dfrac{3\pi}{4}$

11) $\cos \dfrac{\pi}{6}$

12) $\cot \dfrac{\pi}{3}$

13) $\sec -\dfrac{3\pi}{2}$

14) $\tan -\dfrac{2\pi}{3}$

Sketch Each Angle in Standard Position

✎ *Draw the angle with the given measure in standard position.*

1) $140°$

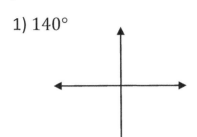

4) $\dfrac{55\pi}{12}$

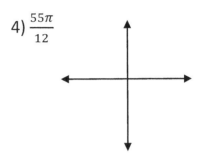

2) $-250°$

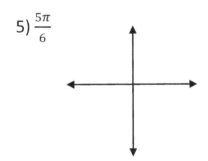

5) $\dfrac{5\pi}{6}$

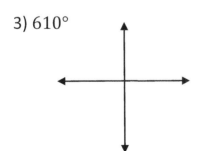

3) $610°$

6) $-\dfrac{13\pi}{6}$

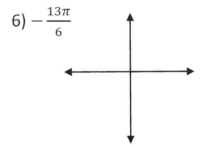

Finding Co-terminal Angles and Reference Angles

Find a conterminal angle between 0◦ and 360◦.

1) $-480°$

2) $680°$

3) $-335°$

4) $-430°$

Find a coterminal angle between 0 and 2π for each given angle.

5) $\dfrac{11\pi}{3}$

6) $-\dfrac{5\pi}{6}$

7) $-\dfrac{2\pi}{45}$

8) $\dfrac{14\pi}{3}$

Find the reference angle.

9)

10)

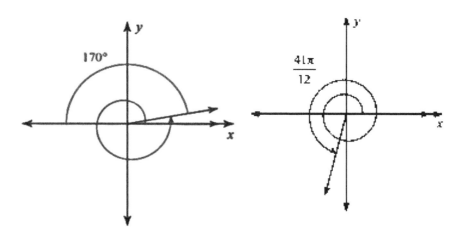

Writing Each Measure in Radians

✍️ *Convert each degree measure into radians.*

1) −120°

2) 220°

3) 160°

4) 920°

5) −200°

6) 230°

7) 265°

8) 20°

9) 420°

10) 30°

11) 297°

12) 500°

13) 504°

14) −130°

15) −260°

16) 423°

17) 440°

18) −190°

19) 250°

20) 350°

Writing Each Measure in Degrees

✏️*Convert each radian measure into degrees.*

1) $\dfrac{\pi}{60}$

2) $\dfrac{12\pi}{30}$

3) $\dfrac{13\pi}{6}$

4) $\dfrac{\pi}{3}$

5) $-\dfrac{10\pi}{9}$

6) $\dfrac{12\pi}{3}$

7) $-\dfrac{16\pi}{3}$

8) $-\dfrac{8\pi}{20}$

9) $\dfrac{5\pi}{6}$

10) $\dfrac{2\pi}{9}$

11) $\dfrac{7\pi}{6}$

12) $\dfrac{15\pi}{60}$

13) $\dfrac{11\pi}{4}$

14) $-\dfrac{22\pi}{11}$

15) $\dfrac{14\pi}{9}$

16) $-\dfrac{41\pi}{60}$

17) $-\dfrac{17\pi}{6}$

18) $\dfrac{32\pi}{18}$

19) $-\dfrac{4\pi}{3}$

20) $\dfrac{5\pi}{9}$

Evaluating Each Trigonometric Function

✍ *Find the exact value of each trigonometric function.*

1) $\cos 315°$

2) $\cot \dfrac{\pi}{6}$

3) $\tan \dfrac{\pi}{6}$

4) $\cot - \dfrac{5\pi}{6}$

5) $\cos \dfrac{2\pi}{3}$

6) $\cos - 240°$

7) $\sin 480°$

8) $\tan 480°$

9) $\cot 390°$

10) $\tan 405°$

✍ Use the given point on the terminal side of angle θ to find the value of the trigonometric function indicated.

11) $\sin \theta; \, (-6, 4)$

12) $\cos \theta; \, (2, -2)$

13) $\cot \theta; \, (-7, \sqrt{15})$

14) $\cos \theta; \, (-2\sqrt{3}, -2)$

15) $\sin \theta; \, (-\sqrt{7}, 3)$

16) $\tan \theta; \, (-11, -2)$

Missing Sides and Angles of a Right Triangle

✍Find the value of each trigonometric ratio as fractions in their simplest form.

1) tan A

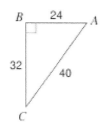

2) sin X

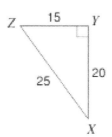

✍Find the missing side. Round answers to the nearest tenth.

3)

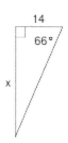

4)

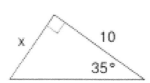

5)

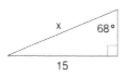

6)

Arc Length and Sector Area

✍ *Find the length of each arc. Round your answers to the nearest tenth.*

1) r = 12 cm, θ = 65∘   3) r = 33 ft, θ = 90∘

2) r = 10 ft, θ = 95∘   4) r = 16 m, θ = 86∘

✍ *Find area of a sector. Do not round.*

5)

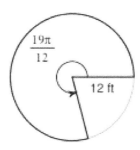

7)

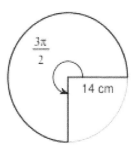

6)

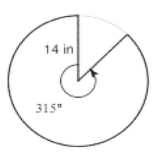

8)

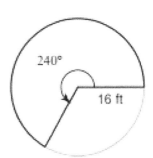

Answers of Worksheets – Chapter 13

Trig Ratios of General Angles

1) $-\frac{1}{2}$

2) $\frac{\sqrt{3}}{2}$

3) $\frac{\sqrt{2}}{2}$

4) $-\frac{1}{2}$

5) 0

6) $\frac{\sqrt{3}}{2}$

7) -2

8) 1

9) $\frac{\sqrt{3}}{2}$

10) $\frac{\sqrt{3}}{3}$

11) Undefined

12) $\sqrt{3}$

Sketch Each Angle in Standard Position

1) 140

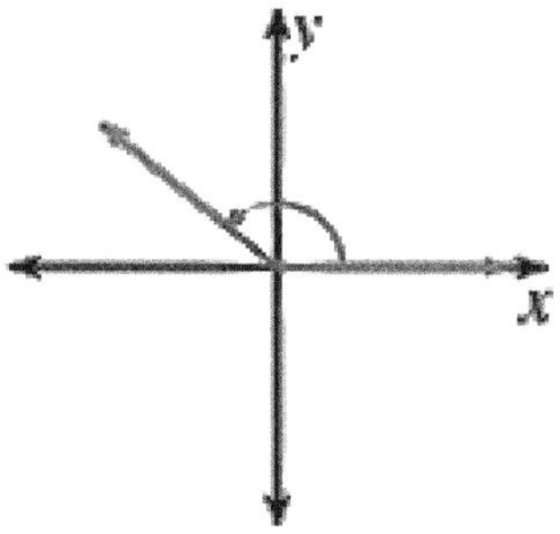

2) -250

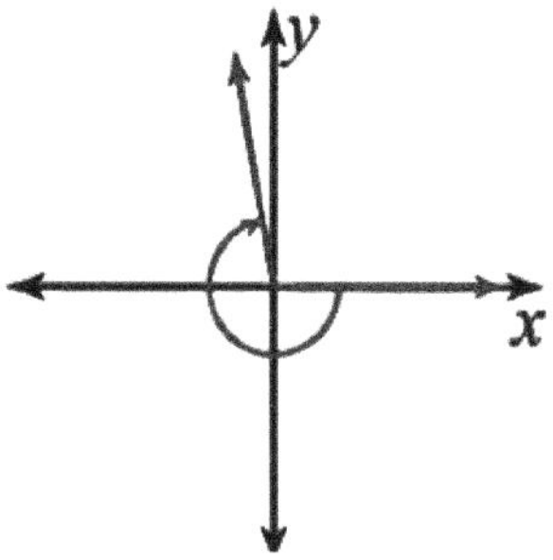

3) 610

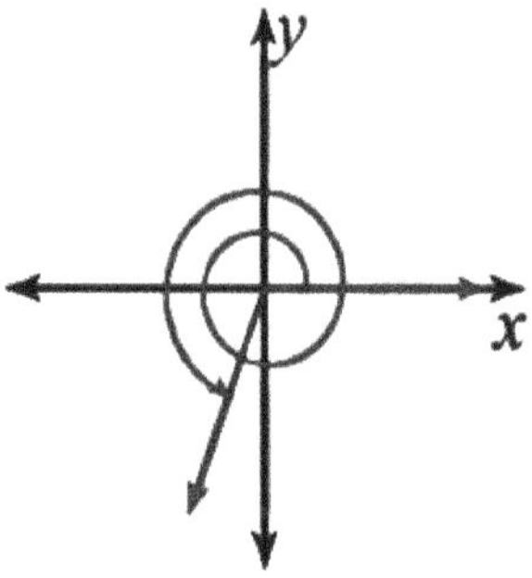

4) $\frac{55\pi}{12}$

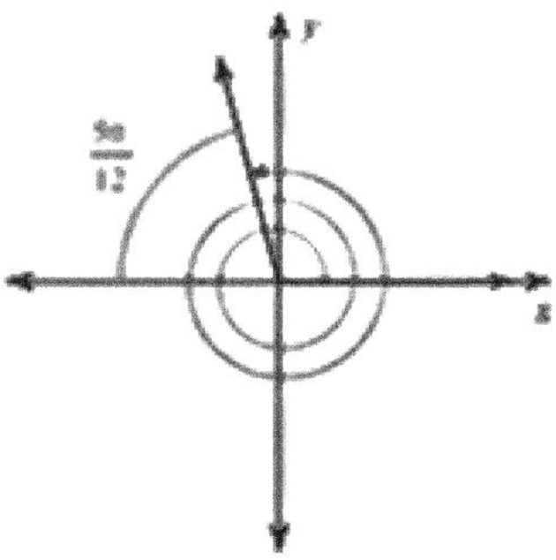

5) $\frac{5\pi}{6}$

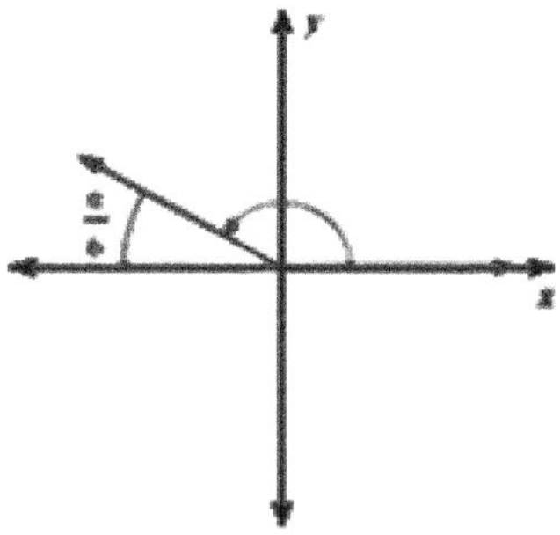

6) $\frac{11\pi}{6}$

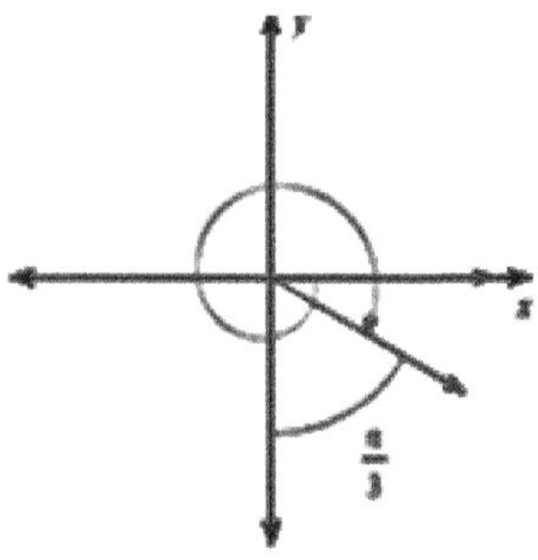

Finding Co–Terminal Angles and Reference Angles

1) $240°$

2) $320°$

3) $25°$

4) $290°$

5) $\frac{5\pi}{3}$

6) $\frac{7\pi}{6}$

7) $\frac{88\pi}{45}$

8) $\frac{2\pi}{3}$

9) $370°$

10) $\frac{5\pi}{12}$

Writing Each Measure in Radians

1) $-\frac{2\pi}{3}$

2) $\frac{11\pi}{9}$

3) $\frac{8\pi}{9}$

4) $\frac{46\pi}{9}$

5) $-\frac{10\pi}{9}$

6) $\frac{23\pi}{18}$

7) $\frac{53\pi}{36}$

8) $\frac{\pi}{9}$

9) $\frac{7\pi}{3}$

10) $\frac{\pi}{6}$

11) $\frac{33\pi}{2}$

12) $\frac{25\pi}{9}$

13) $\frac{14\pi}{5}$

14) $-\frac{13\pi}{18}$

15) $-\frac{13\pi}{9}$

16) $\frac{47\pi}{2}$

17) $\frac{22\pi}{9}$

18) $-\frac{19\pi}{18}$

19) $\frac{25\pi}{18}$

20) $\frac{35\pi}{18}$

Writing Each Measure in Degrees

1) $3°$

2) $72°$

3) $390°$

4) $60°$

5) $-200°$

6) $720°$

7) $-960°$

8) $-72°$

9) $150°$

10) $40°$

11) $210°$

12) $45°$

13) $495°$

14) $-360°$

15) $280°$

16) $-123°$

17) $-510°$

18) $320°$

19) $-240°$

20) $100°$

Evaluating Each Trigonometric Expression

1) $\frac{\sqrt{2}}{2}$

2) $\sqrt{3}$

3) $-\sqrt{3}$

4) $\sqrt{3}$

5) $-\frac{1}{2}$

6) $-\frac{1}{2}$

7) $\frac{\sqrt{3}}{2}$

8) $-\sqrt{3}$

9) $\sqrt{3}$

10) 1

11) $\frac{2\sqrt{13}}{13}$

12) $-\sqrt{2}$

13) $-\frac{7\sqrt{15}}{15}$

14) $-\frac{\sqrt{3}}{2}$

15) $\frac{3}{4}$

16) $\frac{2}{11}$

Missing Sides and Angles of a Right Triangle

1) $\frac{4}{3}$

2) $\frac{3}{5}$

3) 31.4

4) 7.0

5) 16.2

6) 31.1

Arc Length and Sector Area

1) 74 cm

2) 17 ft

3) 52 ft

4) 24 m

5) 114π ft^2

6) $\frac{343\pi}{2}$ in^2

7) 147π cm^2

8) $\frac{512\pi}{3}$ ft^2

Chapter 14: Statistics

Topics that you'll learn in this chapter:

- ✓ Mean, Median, Mode, and Range of the Given Data
- ✓ Box and Whisker Plots
- ✓ Bar Graph
- ✓ Stem– And– Leaf Plot
- ✓ The Pie Graph or Circle Graph
- ✓ Dot and Scatter Plots
- ✓ Probability of Simple Events

Mathematics is no more computation than typing is literature.

– John Allen Paulos

Mean and Median

✎ *Find Mean and Median of the Given Data.*

1) $8, 12, 5, 3, 2$

2) $3, 6, 3, 7, 4, 13$

3) $13, 5, 1, 7, 9$

4) $6, 4, 2, 7, 3, 2$

5) $6, 5, 7, 5, 7, 1, 11$

6) $6, 1, 4, 4, 9, 2, 19$

7) $12, 4, 1, 5, 9, 7, 7, 19$

8) $18, 9, 5, 4, 9, 6, 12$

9) $28, 25, 15, 16, 32, 44, 71$

10) $10, 5, 1, 5, 4, 5, 8, 10$

11) $18, 15, 30, 64, 42, 11$

12) $44, 33, 56, 78, 41, 84$

✎ *Solve.*

13) In a javelin throw competition, five athletics score 56, 58, 63, 57 and 61 meters. What are their Mean and Median?

_____

14) Eva went to shop and bought 3 apples, 5 peaches, 8 bananas, 1 pineapple and 3 melons. What are the Mean and Median of her purchase? _____

Mode and Range

✎ *Find Mode and Rage of the Given Data.*

1) 8, 2, 5, 9, 1, 2

Mode: _____ Range: _____

2) 6, 6, 2, 3, 6, 3, 9, 12

Mode: _____ Range: _____

3) 4, 4, 3, 9, 7, 9, 4, 6, 4

Mode: _____ Range: _____

4) 12, 9, 2, 9, 3, 2, 9, 5

Mode: _____ Range: _____

5) 9, 5, 9, 5, 8, 9, 8

Mode: _____ Range: _____

6) 0, 1, 4, 10, 9, 2, 9, 1, 5, 1

Mode: _____ Range: _____

7) 6, 5, 6, 9, 7, 7, 5, 4, 3, 5

Mode: _____ Range: _____

8) 7, 5, 4, 9, 6, 7, 7, 5, 2

Mode: _____ Range: _____

9) 2, 2, 5, 6, 2, 4, 7, 6, 4, 9

Mode: _____ Range: _____

10) 7, 5, 2, 5, 4, 5, 8, 10

Mode: _____ Range: _____

11) 4, 1, 5, 2, 2, 12, 18, 2

Mode: _____ Range: _____

12) 6, 3, 5, 9, 6, 6, 3, 12

Mode: _____ Range: _____

✎ *Solve.*

13) A stationery sold 12 pencils, 36 red pens, 44 blue pens, 12 notebooks, 18 erasers, 34 rulers and 32 color pencils. What are the Mode and Range for the stationery sells?

Mode: _____   Range: _____

14) In an English test, eight students score 14, 13, 17, 11, 19, 20, 14 and 15. What are their Mode and Range?

_____

Time series

✍ *Use the following Graph to complete the table.*

Day	Distance (km)
1	
2	

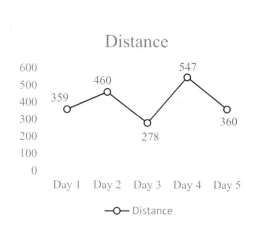

The following table shows the number of births in the US from 2007 to 2012 (in millions).

Year	Number of births (in millions)
2007	4.32
2008	4.25
2009	4.13
2010	4
2011	3.95
2012	3.95

Draw a time series for the table.

Box and Whisker Plot

Make box and whisker plots for the given data.

$$1, 5, 18, 8, 3, 11, 13, 12, 24, 17, 10, 15, 25$$

Bar Graph

Graph the given information as a bar graph.

Day	Sale House
Monday	5
Tuesday	7
Wednesday	9
Thursday	8
Friday	0
Saturday	3
Sunday	4

Dot plots

A survey of "How many pets each person owned?" has these results:

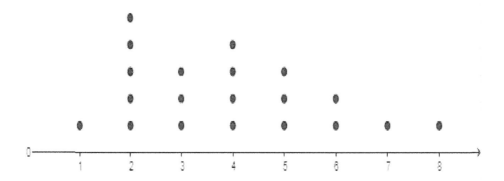

3) What is the most common number of pets?

4) How many people have 3 or less than 3 pets?

5) How many people have more than 6 pets?

Scatter Plots

✎ *Construct a scatter plot.*

x	1	2	3	4	4.5	5
y	5	3.5	4	2	7	1.5

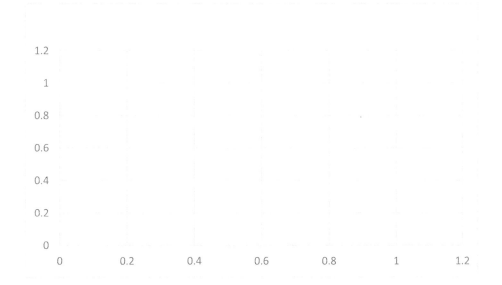

Stem–And–Leaf Plot

✍ *Make stem ad leaf plots for the given data.*

1) $22, 24, 27, 21, 52, 24, 58, 57, 29, 24, 19, 12$

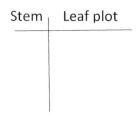

2) $11, 45, 34, 18, 15, 11, 32, 41, 40, 30, 45, 35$

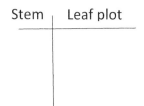

3) $112, 87, 96, 85, 100, 117, 92, 114, 88, 112, 98, 107$

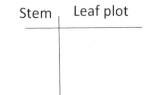

4) $63, 50, 104, 63, 72, 56, 109 \ 63, 75, 59, 63, 108, 79$

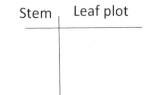

The Pie Graph or Circle Graph

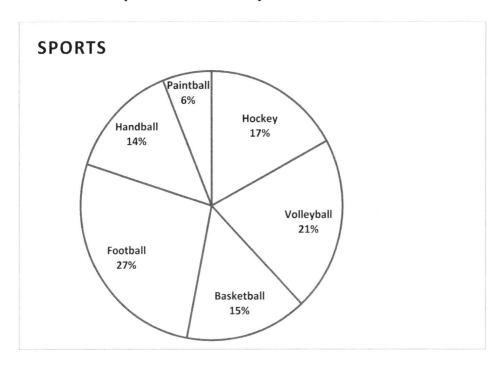

Favorite Sports:

1) What percentage of pie graph is Handball?

2) What percentage of pie graph is Hockey?

3) Which sport is the most?

4) Which sport is the least?

5) What percentage of pie graph is Volleyball?

6) What percentage of pie not football and volleyball?

Probability of Simple Events

✎ *Solve.*

1) A number is chosen at random from 25 to 34. Find the probability of selecting an even number.

2) A number is chosen at random from 21 to 60. Find the probability of selecting multiples of 5.

3) Find the probability of selecting 4 aces from a deck of card.

4) A number is chosen at random from 10 to 19. Find the probability of selecting of 11 and factors of 3.

5) What probability of selecting a ball less than 11 from 40 different bingo balls?

6) Find the probability of not selecting a king from a deck of card.

Experimental Probability

One cube	Frequency
1	6
2	9
3	5
4	7
5	8
6	5

1) Theoretically if you roll a number cube 24 times, how many times would you expect to roll the number two?

2) How many times did you roll the number two in the experiment?

3) Is there any difference between theoretical and experimental probability?

4) What is the theoretical probability for rolling a number greater than 4?

5) What was the experimental probability of rolling a number greater than 3?

Factorials

✎Determine the value for each expression.

1) $5!$

2) $\dfrac{7!}{10!}$

3) $\dfrac{10!}{6!}$

4) $\dfrac{n!}{(n-3)!}$

5) $\dfrac{12!}{8!4!}$

6) $\dfrac{45!}{44!}$

7) $\dfrac{100!}{101!}$

8) $\dfrac{(M+1)!}{(M-1)!}$

9) $\dfrac{15!}{10!}$

10) $\dfrac{28!}{25!}$

11) $\dfrac{0!4!}{1!0!}$

12) $\dfrac{22!}{20!}$

13) $\dfrac{(5.2)!}{(4.2)!}$

14) $7! + 3!$

Permutations

✍ Evaluate each expression.

1) $5 \, _4P_1$

2) $_7P_3$

3) $_8P_5$

4) $12 + \, _{10}P_3$

5) $P(5,3)$

6) $P(6,2)$

7) $(\, _5P_4)$

8) $\frac{1}{2}(\, _{12}P_1)$

9) $_4P_0$

10) $_0P_0$

11) $_4P_4$

12) $_9P_3$

13) How many possible 7–digit telephone numbers are there? Someone left their umbrella on the subway and we need to track them down.

14) With repetition allowed, how many ways can one choose 6 out of 15 things?

Combination

✍ List all possible combinations.

1) 1, 4, 3, 5, taken four at a time

2) A, B, D, taken two at a time

✍ Evaluate each expression.

3) $_4C_1$

4) $_7C_3$

5) $\binom{12}{5}$

6) $3 + \binom{21}{14}$

7) $C(5,3)$

8) $C(6,2)$

9) $5(_{13}C_9)$

10) $\frac{1}{2}(_{12}C_1)$

11) $_5C_0$

12) $_0C_0$

13) $_6C_6$

14) $_{18}C_{17}$

Answers of Worksheets – Chapter 14

Mean and Median

1) Mean: 6, Median: 5

2) Mean: 6, Median: 5

3) Mean: 7, Median: 7

4) Mean: 4, Median: 3.5

5) Mean: 6, Median: 6

6) Mean: 8, Median: 4

7) Mean: 8, Median: 7

8) Mean: 9, Median: 9

9) Mean: 33, Median: 28

10) Mean: 6, Median: 5

11) Mean: 30, Median: 24

12) Mean: 56, Median: 50

13) Mean: 59, Median: 58

14) Mean: 4, Median: 3

Mode and Range

1) Mode: 2, Range: 8

2) Mode: 6, Range: 10

3) Mode: 4, Range: 6

4) Mode: 9, Range: 10

5) Mode: 9, Range: 4

6) Mode: 1, Range: 10

7) Mode: 5, Range: 6

8) Mode: 7, Range: 7

9) Mode: 2, Range: 7

10) Mode: 5, Range: 8

11) Mode: 2, Range: 17

12) Mode: 6, Range: 9

13) Mode: 12, Range: 32

14) Mode: 14, Range: 9

Time Series

Day	Distance (km)
1	359
2	460
3	278
4	547
5	360

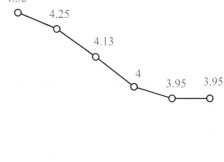

Number of Births

Box and Whisker Plots

1, 3, 5, 8, 10, 11, 12, 13, 15, 17, 18, 24, 25

Maximum: 25, Minimum: 1, Q_1: 6.5, Q_2: 12, Q_3: 17.5

Dot plots

1) *11*　　　　　　3) *2*　　　　　　5) *2*

2) *5*　　　　　　4) *9*

Bar Graph

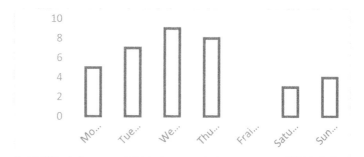

Scatter Plots

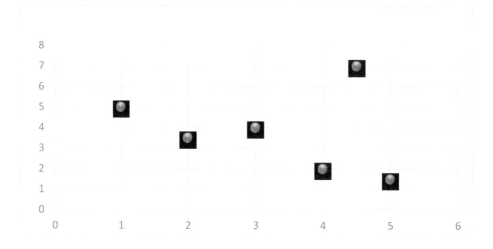

Stem–And–Leaf Plot

1)

Stem	leaf
1	2 9
2	1 2 4 4 4 7 9
5	2 7 8

2)

Stem	leaf
1	1 1 5 8
3	0 2 4 5
4	0 1 5 5

3)

Stem	leaf
8	5 7 8
9	2 6 8
10	0 7
11	2 2 4 7

4)

Stem	leaf
5	0 6 9
6	3 3 3 3
7	2 5 9
10	4 8 9

The Pie Graph or Circle Graph

1) 14%

2) Football

3) Paintball

4) 17%

5) 21%

6) 52%

Probability of simple events

1) $\frac{1}{2}$

2) $\frac{1}{5}$

3) $\frac{1}{13}$

4) $\frac{2}{5}$

5) $\frac{1}{4}$

6) $\frac{12}{13}$

Experimental Probability

1) 4

2) 9

3) yes

4) 1/3

5) 1/2

Factorials

1) 120

2) 336

3) 5,040

4) $n(n-1)(n-2)$

5) 495

6) 45

7) $\frac{1}{100}$

8) $M(M-1)$

9) 360,360

10) 19,656

11) 24

12) 462   13) 5.2   14) 5046

Permutations

1) 20	5) 60	9) 1	13) 10^7
2) 210	6) 30	10) 1	14) 15^6
3) 6720	7) 120	11) 24	
4) 732	8) 6	12) 504	

Combination

1) 1435	6) 116,283	11) 6
2) AB, AD, BD	7) 10	12) 1
3) 4	8) 15	13) 1
4) 35	9) 715	14) 18
5) 792	10) 495	

GRE Math Test Review

The graduate record exam or GRE is the most commonly used admission test for grad schools. In essence, it is a broad and quick assessment of your quantitative reasoning abilities, analytical writing and verbal reasoning.

Most often we tend to be good at one or two of these three aspects, yet we unconsciously use all of them every day to reach a decision. It is mainly used by the schools to determine if you are the best fit for the program you want to enroll for. To keep up with the changing methods and nature of analytics, the GRE test were changed in 2011.

The GRE is divided into three major segments. Number one is the analytical writing. The second one is the verbal segment. The third segment is the quantitative reasoning section. This section gauges your algebra, data analysis, geometry and arithmetic. It also tests your ability to form conclusions in quantitative reasoning.

In a GRE assessment test all questions are weighted the same. You also have to keep in mind that the more difficult questions are randomly thrown around in the test. You can choose to skip over the more challenging tasks and ace out the simpler questions in the tests first.

There are 20 Mathematics questions on GRE. The Quantitative Reasoning section of the GRE General Test contains four types of questions:

- ✓ Quantitative Comparison Questions
- ✓ Multiple-choice Questions — Select One Answer Choice

✓ Multiple-choice Questions — Select One or More Answer Choices

✓ Numeric Entry Questions

GRE uses the computer-adaptive technology. It means that the test will "choose" the difficulty level of your next section based on your success rate in the prior section. Therefore, your result in the first section drives the difficulty level of the next section.

GRE does NOT permit the use of personal calculators on the Math portion of placement test. However, it provides an onscreen calculator for students to use for quantitative reasoning questions.

In this section, there are two complete GRE Quantitative Reasoning Tests. Take these tests to see what score you'll be able to receive on a real GRE test.

The hardest arithmetic to master is that which enables us to count our blessings. ~Eric Hoffer

Time to Test

Time to refine your skill with a practice examination

Take a practice GRE Math Test to simulate the test day experience. After you've finished, score your test using the answer key.

Before You Start

- You'll need a pencil, a calculator and a timer to take the test.
- For each question, there are five possible answers. Choose which one is best.
- It's okay to guess. There is no penalty for wrong answers.
- Use the answer sheet provided to record your answers.
- After you've finished the test, review the answer key to see where you went wrong.

Good Luck!

GRE Math Practice Test Answer Sheets

Remove (or photocopy) these answer sheets and use them to complete the practice tests.

GRE Practice Test

Section 1		Section 2	
1	Ⓐ Ⓑ Ⓒ Ⓓ Ⓔ	1	Ⓐ Ⓑ Ⓒ Ⓓ Ⓔ
2	Ⓐ Ⓑ Ⓒ Ⓓ Ⓔ	2	Ⓐ Ⓑ Ⓒ Ⓓ Ⓔ
3	Ⓐ Ⓑ Ⓒ Ⓓ Ⓔ	3	Ⓐ Ⓑ Ⓒ Ⓓ Ⓔ
4	Ⓐ Ⓑ Ⓒ Ⓓ Ⓔ	4	Ⓐ Ⓑ Ⓒ Ⓓ Ⓔ
5	Ⓐ Ⓑ Ⓒ Ⓓ Ⓔ	5	Ⓐ Ⓑ Ⓒ Ⓓ Ⓔ
6	Ⓐ Ⓑ Ⓒ Ⓓ Ⓔ	6	Ⓐ Ⓑ Ⓒ Ⓓ Ⓔ
7	Ⓐ Ⓑ Ⓒ Ⓓ Ⓔ	7	Ⓐ Ⓑ Ⓒ Ⓓ Ⓔ
8	Ⓐ Ⓑ Ⓒ Ⓓ Ⓔ	8	Ⓐ Ⓑ Ⓒ Ⓓ Ⓔ
9	Ⓐ Ⓑ Ⓒ Ⓓ Ⓔ	9	Ⓐ Ⓑ Ⓒ Ⓓ Ⓔ
10	Ⓐ Ⓑ Ⓒ Ⓓ Ⓔ	10	Ⓐ Ⓑ Ⓒ Ⓓ Ⓔ
11	Ⓐ Ⓑ Ⓒ Ⓓ Ⓔ	11	Ⓐ Ⓑ Ⓒ Ⓓ Ⓔ
12	Ⓐ Ⓑ Ⓒ Ⓓ Ⓔ	12	Ⓐ Ⓑ Ⓒ Ⓓ Ⓔ
13	Ⓐ Ⓑ Ⓒ Ⓓ Ⓔ	13	Ⓐ Ⓑ Ⓒ Ⓓ Ⓔ
14	Ⓐ Ⓑ Ⓒ Ⓓ Ⓔ	14	Ⓐ Ⓑ Ⓒ Ⓓ Ⓔ
15	Ⓐ Ⓑ Ⓒ Ⓓ Ⓔ	15	Ⓐ Ⓑ Ⓒ Ⓓ Ⓔ
16	Ⓐ Ⓑ Ⓒ Ⓓ Ⓔ	16	Ⓐ Ⓑ Ⓒ Ⓓ Ⓔ
17	Ⓐ Ⓑ Ⓒ Ⓓ Ⓔ	17	Ⓐ Ⓑ Ⓒ Ⓓ Ⓔ
18	Ⓐ Ⓑ Ⓒ Ⓓ Ⓔ	18	Ⓐ Ⓑ Ⓒ Ⓓ Ⓔ
19	Ⓐ Ⓑ Ⓒ Ⓓ Ⓔ	19	Ⓐ Ⓑ Ⓒ Ⓓ Ⓔ
20	Ⓐ Ⓑ Ⓒ Ⓓ Ⓔ	20	Ⓐ Ⓑ Ⓒ Ⓓ Ⓔ

GRE Practice Test 1

Quantitative Reasoning

Section - 1

❖ **20 Questions.**

❖ **Total time for this test: 35 Minutes.**

❖ **You may use a basic calculator on this Section.**

Administered *Month Year*

1) 5 percent of x is equal to 4 percent of y, where x and y are positive numbers.

Quantity A	Quantity B
x	y

A. Quantity A is greater.

B. Quantity B is greater.

C. The two quantities are equal.

D. The relationship cannot be determined from the information given.

2) Emma and Sophia have a family business. The profit of their business will be divided between Emma and Sophia in the ratio 4 to 5 respectively.

Quantity A	Quantity B
The money Emma receives when the profit is $540.	The money Sophia receives when the profit is $432.

A. Quantity A is greater.

B. Quantity B is greater.

C. The two quantities are equal.

D. The relationship cannot be determined from the information given.

3) a and b are real numbers. $b < a$

Quantity A	**Quantity B**
$|b - a|$	$|a - b|$

A. Quantity A is greater.

B. Quantity B is greater.

C. The two quantities are equal.

D. The relationship cannot be determined from the information given.

4) x is an integer greater than zero?

Quantity A	**Quantity B**
$\frac{1}{x} + x$	8

A. Quantity A is greater.

B. Quantity B is greater.

C. The two quantities are equal.

D. The relationship cannot be determined from the information given.

5)

Quantity A	**Quantity B**
The least prime factor of 77	The least prime factor of 210

A. Quantity A is greater.

B. Quantity B is greater.

C. The two quantities are equal.

D. The relationship cannot be determined from the information given.

6) The volume of a sphere with diameter of length 7 is how many times the volume of sphere with diameter of length $\sqrt{7}$? (Volume of a sphere = $\frac{4}{3}\pi r^3$)

A. $\sqrt{7}$

B. 7

C. 10

D. $10\sqrt{7}$

E. $7\sqrt{7}$

7) The average of x , y and 6 is 6 and $x - y = -8$. What is the value of $x \times y$?

A. 10

B. -10

C. 20

D. -20

E. 0

8) The surface area of a cylinder is $168\pi\ cm^2$. If its height is 8 cm, what is the radius of the cylinder?

A. 10 cm

B. 11 cm

C. 14 cm

D. 6 cm

E. 7 cm

9) In the xy-plane, the point (5,4) and (4,3) are on line A. Which of the following equations of lines is parallel to line A?

A. $y = 3x$

B. $y = 10$

C. $y = \frac{x}{2}$

D. $y = 2x$

E. $y = x$

10) If $y = 3^4$ then what is the value of $y^{\sqrt{y}}$?

A. 3

B. 3^4

C. 3^8

D. 3^{36}

E. 3^{32}

11) What is the solution of the following system of equations?

$$\begin{cases} -\dfrac{x}{2} + \dfrac{y}{6} = 1 \\ -\dfrac{5y}{6} + 3x = 2 \end{cases}$$

A. $x = 48, y = 183$

D. $x = 22, y = 50$

B. $x = 50, y = 20$

E. $x = 14, y = 48$

C. $x = 20, y = 50$

12) The average weight of 16 girls in a class is 65 kg and the average weight of 34 boys in the same class is 67 kg. What is the average weight of all the 50 students in that class?

A. 60

C. 66.68

E. 62.20

B. 66.36

D. 66.90

13) If 80 % of A is 20 % of B, then B is what percent of A?

A. 4 %

C. 200 %

E. 800 %

B. 40 %

D. 400 %

14) If $(x - 4)^3 = 8$ which of the following could be the value of $(x - 5)(x - 3)$?

A. 1

C. 5

E. -3

B. 3

D. -1

15) If $(x - 3)^2 + 1 > 3x - 1$, then x can equal to which of the following?

A. 2

C. 9

E. 4

B. 5

D. 3

A library has 700 books that include Mathematics, Physics, Chemistry, English and History.

Use following graph to answer questions 16 to 18.

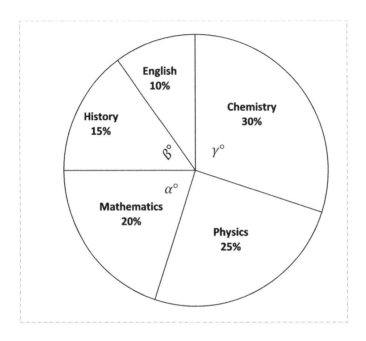

16) What is the product of the number of Mathematics and number of English books?

A. 1,168   C. 6,460   E. 4,112

B. 9,800   D. 7,640

17) The librarians decided to move some of the books in the Mathematics section to Chemistry section. How many books are in the Chemistry section if now $\gamma = \frac{2}{5}\alpha$?

A. 80   C. 250   E. 180

B. 100   D. 200

18) What are the values of angle α and β ?

    A. $90°, 54°$ C. $110°, 55°$ E. $72°, 36°$

    B. $110°, 46°$ D. $72°, 54°$

19) Let r and p be constants. If $x^2 + 8x + r$ factors into $(x + 3)(x + p)$, the values of r and p respectively are?

    A. $15, 5$ C. $6, 3$

    B. $5, 15$ D. $3, 6$

    E. The answer cannot be found from the information given.

20) In how many ways can 5 cards be placed in 4 positions if any cards can be placed in any position?

    A. 5   C. 15   E. 120

    B. 10   D. 30

STOP

This is the End of this Test. You may check your work on this section if you still have time.

GRE Practice Test 1

Quantitative Reasoning

Section - 2

❖ **20 Questions.**

❖ **Total time for this test: 35 Minutes.**

❖ **You may use a basic calculator on this Section.**

Administered *Month Year*

1) n is a natural number and $\frac{1}{2^n} < \frac{1}{8}$

Quantity A	Quantity B
3	n

A. Quantity A is greater.

B. Quantity B is greater.

C. The two quantities are equal.

D. The relationship cannot be determined from the information given.

2) The average of 2, 6, and x is 3.

Quantity A	Quantity B
x	average of $x, x - 2, x + 1, 2x$

A. Quantity A is greater.

B. Quantity B is greater.

C. The two quantities are equal.

D. The relationship cannot be determined from the information given.

3)

Quantity A	Quantity B
$(-3)^4$	3^4

A. Quantity A is greater.

B. Quantity B is greater.

C. The two quantities are equal.

D. The relationship cannot be determined from the information given.

4)

$$\frac{3}{5} < x < \frac{4}{6}$$

Quantity A	**Quantity B**
x	$\frac{5}{8}$

A. Quantity A is greater.

B. Quantity B is greater.

C. The two quantities are equal.

D. The relationship cannot be determined from the information given.

5)

Quantity A	**Quantity B**
$\frac{x^5}{5}$	$\left(\frac{x}{5}\right)^5$

A. Quantity A is greater.

B. Quantity B is greater.

C. The two quantities are equal.

D. The relationship cannot be determined from the information given.

6)

Quantity A	**Quantity B**
$10 + 8 \times (-3) - [4 + 32 \times 5] \div 4$	$[6 \times (-24) + 8] - (-4) + [4 \times 5] \div 2$

A. Quantity A is greater.

B. Quantity B is greater.

C. The two quantities are equal.

D. The relationship cannot be determined from the information given.

7) The length of a rectangle is $\frac{5}{4}$ times its width. If the width is 12, what is the perimeter of this rectangle?

    A. 32   C. 54   E. 108

    B. 48   D. 144

8) The ratio of boys and girls in a class is 7:4. If there are 33 students in the class, how many more boys should be enrolled to make the ratio 1:1?

    A. 8   C. 12   E. 28

    B. 10   D. 14

9) If 120 % of a number is 72, then what is 90 % of that number?

    A. 54   C. 60   E. 55

    B. 40   D. 75

10) f $|a| < 2$ then which of the following is true? $(b > 0)$?

    I. $-b < ba < b$

    II. $-a < a^2 < a \quad if \ a < 0$

    III. $-7 < 2a - 3 < 1$

    A. I only   C. I and III only   E. I, II and III

    B. II only   D. III only

11) Removing which of the following numbers will change the average of the numbers to 7?   2, 3, 6, 7, 10, 13

    A. 2   C. 6   E. 13

    B. 3   D. 10

12) The marked price of a computer is D dollar. Its price decreased by 40% in January and later increased by 10 % in February. What is the final price of the computer in D dollar?

A. 0.60 D

B. 0.66 D

C. 0.50 D

D. 1.20 D

E. 1.40 D

13) In the following figure, what is the perimeter of Δ ABC if the area of Δ ADC is 10?

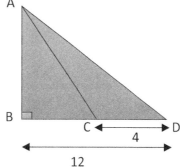

A. 37.5

B. 21

C. 15

D. 30

E. The answer cannot be determined from the information given

14) A line l is parallel to the x-axis and passes through the point $(-4, 5)$. What is the slope of the line (m) and its y-intercept?

A. $m = \infty$, y-intercept= 5

B. $m = \infty$, y-intercept= -4

C. $m = 0$,y-intercept= -4

D. $m = 0$, y-intercept= 5

E. $m = -4$, y-intercept= 5

15) What is the product of all possible values of x in the following equation?

$$|x - 2x - 6 + 8| = 3$$

A. 5

B. -5

C. 6

D. -6

E. 0

Questions 16 to 18 are based on the following data

Number of clothes sold in a clothing store

16) Between which two of the months shown was there a twenty percent increase in the number of pants sold?

    A. January and February   D. April and May

    B. February and March   E. May and June

    C. March and April

17) During the six-month period shown, what is the mean number of shirts and median number of shoes per month?

    A. 25, 147.5   D. 30, 147.5

    B. 149, 25   E. 30, 25

    C. 149, 30

18) How many shoes need to be added in April until the ratio of number of pants to number of shoes in April equals to five-twelfth of this ratio in May?

    A. 20   C. 25   E. 40

    B. 30   D. 35

19) A 8 cm by 15cm rectangle is inscribed in a circle. What is the circumference of the circle?

    A. 5π cm   C. 12π cm   E. 26π cm

    B. 6.55π cm   D. 17π cm

20) In the following figure, $ABCD$ is a rectangle, and E and F are points on AD and DC, respectively and $DE = 6$ and $DF = 4$. The area of ΔBED is 12, and the area of ΔBDF is 16. What is the perimeter of the rectangle?

    A. 20

    B. 22

    C. 32

    D. 24

    E. 44

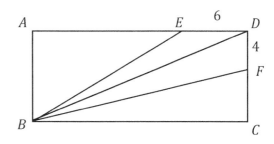

STOP

This is the End of this Test. You may check your work on this section if you still have time.

GRE Practice Test 2

Quantitative Reasoning

Section - 1

❖ **20 Questions.**

❖ **Total time for this test: 35 Minutes**.

❖ **You may use a basic calculator on this Section.**

Administered *Month Year*

1) x is a positive integer greater than 1?

Quantity A	Quantity B
$\sqrt{x+1}$	$\sqrt{x+\sqrt{x}}$

A. Quantity A is greater.

B. Quantity B is greater.

C. The two quantities are equal.

D. The relationship cannot be determined from the information given.

2) x and y are positive numbers.

Quantity A	Quantity B
$x^2 - 2xy$	$(x-y)^2$

A. Quantity A is greater.

B. Quantity B is greater.

C. The two quantities are equal.

D. The relationship cannot be determined from the information given.

3)

$$x^2 - 4x - 12 = 0$$

Quantity A	Quantity B
x	5

A. Quantity A is greater.

B. Quantity B is greater.

C. The two quantities are equal.

D. The relationship cannot be determined from the information given.

4) In the xy-plane, two points $(p, 0)$ and $(0, q)$ are on a line with

equation $y = \frac{2}{3}x + 14$.

Quantity A	**Quantity B**
p	q

A. Quantity A is greater.

B. Quantity B is greater.

C. The two quantities are equal.

D. The relationship cannot be determined from the

information given.

5) $x > y$

Quantity A	**Quantity B**
$|x^2 + y|$	$|x^2 - y|$

A. Quantity A is greater.

B. Quantity B is greater.

C. The two quantities are equal.

D. The relationship cannot be determined from the

information given.

6) Mr. Jones obtained a $17,000 loan at a simple annual interest

rate of p percent. After two years, he paid $15,470 to repay the

loan and its interest. What is the value of p?

A. 2.5   C. 4.5   E. 7

B. 3.5   D. 6

7) A ladder leans against a wall forming a 60° angle between the ground and the ladder. If the bottom of the ladder is 42 feet away from the wall, how long is the ladder?

A. 84 feet   C. 21 feet   E. 6 feet

B. 42 feet   D. 7 feet

8) The mean of 60 test scores was calculated as 77. But it turned out that one of the scores was misread as 64 but it was 46. What is the mean?

A. 77   C. 76.70   E. 77.70

B. 76.30   D. 77.30

9) Two dice are thrown simultaneously, what is the probability of getting a sum of 6 or 4?

A. $\frac{10}{24}$ C. $\frac{5}{6}$ E. $\frac{5}{36}$

B. $\frac{2}{3}$ D. $\frac{2}{9}$

10) If $(2^{6x})(64) = 2^{2y}$, where x and y are integers, what is the value of y in terms of x?

A. $3x$ C. $3x + 2$ E. $6x + 4$

B. $6x$ D. $3x + 81$

11) The ratio of boys to girls in a school is 2:4. If there are 600 students in a school, how many boys are in the school.

A. 540   C. 300   E. 200

B. 360   D. 280

12) What is the area of the following equilateral triangle if the side

AB = 10 cm?

A. $25\sqrt{3}$ cm²

B. $50\sqrt{3}$ cm²

C. $10\sqrt{3}$ cm²

D. $\sqrt{75}$ cm²

E. 75 cm²

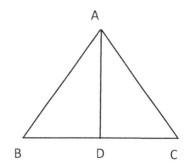

13) If 90% of x equal to 30% of 30, then what is the value of

$(x + 3)^2$?

A. 1.69   C. 8.1   E. 169

B. 9   D. 27

14) The perimeter of a rectangular yard is 120 meters. What is its

length if its width is twice its length?

A. 10 meters   C. 20 meters   E. 36 meters

B. 18 meters   D. 24 meters

15) What is the value of x in the following system of equations?

$$6x + 3y = -3$$
$$2x + 5y = 11$$

A. -1 C. -2 E. 8

B. 1   D. 4

Questions 16, 17 are based on the following data

Types of air pollutions in 10 cities of a country

Type of Pollution	Number of Cities									
A	■	■	■	■	■	■	■	■		
B	■	■	■	■						
C	■	■	■							
D	■	■	■	■	■	■	■	■	■	
E	■	■	■	■	■					
	1	2	3	4	5	6	7	8	9	10

16) If a is the mean (average) of the number of cities in each pollution type category, b is the mode, and c is the median of the number of cities in each pollution type category, then which of the following must be true?

A. $a < b < c$ C. $a = c$ E. $a = b = c$

B. $b < a < c$ D. $b < c = a$

17) How many cities should be added to type of pollutions C until the ratio of cities in type of pollution C to cities in type of pollution A will be 0.750?

A. 2   C. 4   E. 6

B. 3   D. 5

18) Four years ago, Amy was x times as old as Mike was. If Mike is

8 years old now, how old is Amy in terms of x?

A. $4x$ C. $5x - 8$ E. $4x + 8$

B. $10x$ D. $4x + 4$

19) From the figure, which of the following must be true? (figure

not drawn to scale)

A. $y = z$

B. $y = 6x$

C. $y \geq x$

D. $y + 6x = z$

E. $y > x$

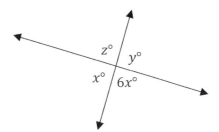

20) The average of 6 numbers is 14. The average of 4 of those

numbers is 10. What is the average of the other two numbers?

A. 10   C. 14   E. 22

B. 12   D. 16

STOP

This is the End of this Test. You may check your work on this section if you still have time.

GRE Practice Test 2

Quantitative Reasoning

Section - 2

❖ **20 Questions.**

❖ **Total time for this test: 35 Minutes.**

❖ **You may use a basic calculator on this Section.**

Administered *Month Year*

1) x is a positive number.

Quantity A	Quantity B
x^{20}	x^{30}

A. Quantity A is greater.

B. Quantity B is greater.

C. The two quantities are equal.

D. The relationship cannot be determined from the information given.

2)

Quantity A	Quantity B
$(1.88)^3(1.88)^7$	$(1.88)^{10}$

A. Quantity A is greater.

B. Quantity B is greater.

C. The two quantities are equal.

D. The relationship cannot be determined from the information given.

3)

Quantity A	Quantity B
radius of a circle with the area of 81	$\dfrac{9}{\sqrt{\pi}}$

A. Quantity A is greater.

B. Quantity B is greater.

C. The two quantities are equal.

D. The relationship cannot be determined from the information given.

4) $5 < x < 9$

Quantity A	Quantity B
$\dfrac{x+4}{4}$	$\dfrac{x^2-25}{x^2-5x}$

A. Quantity A is greater.

B. Quantity B is greater.

C. The two quantities are equal.

D. The relationship cannot be determined from the information given.

5) A right cylinder with radius 2 inches has volume 75π cubic inches.

Quantity A	Quantity B
the height of the cylinder	10 inches

A. Quantity A is greater.

B. Quantity B is greater.

C. The two quantities are equal.

D. The relationship cannot be determined from the information given.

6) If the average (arithmetic mean) of numbers in Set B is 9, what is the average of numbers in Set A?

Set A:$\{9, 5, 12, 8, 6, x, y\}$; Set B: $\{5, 8, x, y\}$

Write your answer in the box below.

7) What are the solutions of the following equation?

$$(x^2 + x)(x - 4) = 6x$$

A. 0

C. $0, -3, -5$

E. No solution

B. $0, 3 - \sqrt{3}, \sqrt{3} + 3$

D. $0, -2, 5$

8) If a and b are two positive natural numbers and a is 40% less than b, what is the value of $(\frac{a}{b})^2$?

A. 0.6

C. $\dfrac{10}{6}$

E. 1.69

B. 0.36

D. $\dfrac{100}{36}$

9) In two successive years, the population of a town is increased by 25% and 40%. What percent of the population is increased after two years?

A. 100%

C. 75%

E. 15%

B. 25%

D. 65%

10) From the figure, which of the following must be true? (figure not drawn to scale)

A. $y = z$

B. $y = 6x$

C. $y \geq x$

D. $y + 5x = z$

E. $y > x$

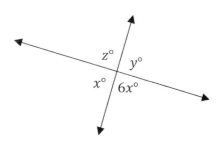

11) A certain experiment has possible mutually exclusive outcomes and have probabilities $n, \frac{n}{2}, \frac{3n}{4}$, respectively. What is the value of n?

A. $\frac{4}{9}$

B. $\frac{7}{9}$

C. $\frac{2}{5}$

D. $\frac{1}{2}$

E. $\frac{1}{4}$

12) The average of five consecutive numbers is 36. What is the smallest number?

A. 38

B. 36

C. 34

D. 12

E. 8

13) A chemical solution contains 4% alcohol. If there is 36 ml of alcohol, what is the volume of the solution?

A. 240 ml

B. 480 ml

C. 800 ml

D. 1,200 ml

E. 2,400 ml

14) The average of five numbers is 22. If a sixth number 52 is added, then, what is the new average?

A. 25

B. 26

C. 27

D. 28

E. 36

15) If n is even, which of the following cannot be odd?

Select all that apply.

A. $n + 11$

B. $n^2 + 2(n + 1)$

C. $7n$

D. $3n^2 + 5n$

E. $n^3 + 3n + 1$

F. $4(n + 3)$

Questions 16 to 18 are based on the following data

The result of a research shows the number of men and women in four cities of a country.

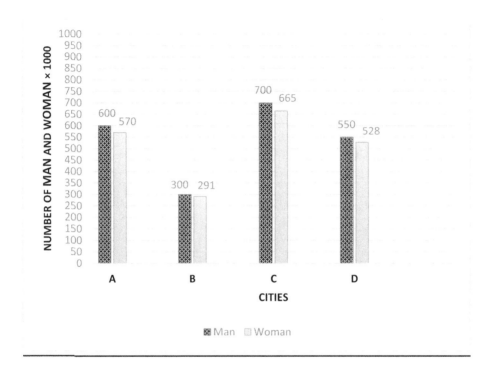

16) What's the ratio of percentage of men in city C to percentage of women in city B?

A. 0.10   C. 0.99   E. 1.00

B. 0.01   D. 1.01

17) What's the minimum ratio of woman to man in the four cities?

A. 0.97   C. 0.95   E. 0.96

B. 0.98   D. 0.99

18) How many women should be added to city D until the ratio of women to men will be 1.3?

   A. 122   C. 148   E. 135

   B. 187   D. 192

19) In the following figure, $ABCD$ is a rectangle. If $a = \sqrt{2}$, and $b = 2a$, find the area of the shaded region. (the shaded region is a trapezoid)

   A. 3

   B. 2

   C. $\sqrt{2}$

   D. $2\sqrt{2}$

   E. $4\sqrt{2}$

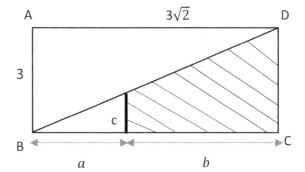

20) Two cars are 300 miles apart. They both drive in a straight line toward each other. If Car A drives at 68 mph and Car B drives at 82mph, then how many miles apart will they be exactly 40 minutes before they meet?

   A. 60 miles   C. 100 miles   E. 120 miles

   B. 80 miles   D. 110 miles

STOP

This is the End of this Test. You may check your work on this section if you still have time.

Answers and Explanations
GRE Math Practice Tests

Answer Key

❋ Now, it's time to review your results to see where you went wrong and what areas you need to improve!

GRE Math Practice Test 1

Section 1		Section 2	
1	B	1	B
2	C	2	C
3	C	3	C
4	D	4	D
5	A	5	A
6	E	6	A
7	C	7	C
8	D	8	D
9	E	9	A
10	D	10	D
11	E	11	C
12	B	12	B
13	D	13	D
14	B	14	D
15	C	15	B
16	B	16	D
17	B	17	C
18	D	18	B
19	A	19	D
20	A	20	D

GRE Math Practice Test 2

Section 1		Section 2	
1	B	1	D
2	B	2	C
3	B	3	C
4	B	4	A
5	D	5	A
6	C	6	9
7	A	7	D
8	C	8	B
9	D	9	C
10	C	10	D
11	E	11	A
12	A	12	C
13	E	13	C
14	C	14	C
15	C	15	B, C, F
16	C	16	D
17	B	17	C
18	D	18	B
19	D	19	E
20	E	20	C

How to score **your** test

GRE scores are broken down by three sections: Quantitative Reasoning, Verbal Reasoning, and Analytical Writing.

For the Quantitative Reasoning and Verbal Reasoning, the score scale is 130-170, in one-point increments. The scores these two sections will appear on your computer screen immediately after you finish the test. The total scaled score for GRE test is the sum of the scores for these two sections. You will also receive a percentile score of between 1-99% that compares your test scores with other test takers.

The Analytical Writing section has a score range of 0-6, in half-point increments, and it is provided separately. This score will be available online about 10 days taking the test.

To find your score on the practice tests on this book, your raw score has to be converted to a scaled score (the official score you receive). Your raw score is the number of points you earned on the exam (you get a point for each question you answer correctly, and no points are deducted for incorrect answers).

Use the next table to convert your raw score to scaled score.

GRE Quantitative Reasoning Scaled Scores

Raw Score	Scaled Score	Raw Score	Scaled Score	Raw Score	Scaled Score	Raw Score	Scaled Score
0	130						
1	131	11	141	21	151	31	161
2	132	12	142	22	152	32	162
3	133	13	143	23	153	33	163
4	134	14	144	24	154	34	164
5	135	15	145	25	155	35	165
6	136	16	146	26	156	36	166
7	137	17	147	27	157	37	167
8	138	18	148	28	158	38	168
9	139	19	149	29	159	39	169
10	140	20	150	30	160	40	170

Answers and Explanations

GRE Quantitative Reasoning

Practice Tests 1

Section 1

1) Answer: B.

5% of x = 4% of $y \rightarrow 0.05\ x\ =\ 0.04\ y \rightarrow x = \frac{0.04}{0.05}y \rightarrow x = \frac{4}{5}y$,

therefore, y is bigger than x.

2) Answer: C.

The profit of their business will be divided between Emma and

Sophia in the ratio 4 to 5 respectively. Therefore, Emma receives $\frac{4}{9}$

of the whole profile and Sophia receives $\frac{5}{9}$ of the whole profile.

Quantity A: The money Emma receives when the profit is $540

equals: $\frac{4}{9} \times 540 = 240$

Quantity B: The money Sophia receives when the profit is $430

equals: $\frac{5}{9} \times 432 = 240$

The two quantities are equal.

3) Answer: C.

Choose different values for a and b and find the values of quantity

A and quantity B. $a = 3$ and $b = 2$, then:

Quantity A: $|2 - 3| = |-1| = 1$

Quantity B: $|3 - 2| = |1| = 1$

The two quantities are equal.

$a = 2$ and $b = -3$, then:

Quantity A: $|-3 - 2| = |-5| = 5$

Quantity B: $|2 - (-3)| = |2 + 3| = 5$

The two quantities are equal. Any other values of a and b provide

the same answer

4) Answer: D.

Choose different values for x and find the value of quantity A.

$x = 1$, then: Quantity A: $\frac{1}{x} + x = \frac{1}{1} + 1 = 2$

Quantity B is greater

$x = 8$, then:

Quantity A: $\frac{1}{x} + x = \frac{1}{8} + 8 = 8 + 0.125 = 8.125$

Quantity A is greater

The relationship cannot be determined from the information

given.

5) Answer: A.

prime factoring of 77 is: 7×11

prime factoring of 210 is: $2 \times 3 \times 5 \times 7$

Quantity A = 7 and Quantity B = 2

6) Answer: E.

$$V_1 = \frac{4\pi}{3}\left(\frac{7}{2}\right)^3$$

$$V_2 = \frac{4\pi}{3}\left(\frac{\sqrt{7}}{2}\right)^3 \quad \rightarrow \quad \frac{V_1}{V_2} = 7\sqrt{7}$$

7) Answer: C.

$$\text{average} = \frac{sum\ of\ terms}{number\ of\ terms} \rightarrow \frac{x+y+6}{3} = 6 \rightarrow x + y = 12$$

$$\begin{cases} x + y = 12 \\ x - y = -8 \end{cases} \quad \text{add both equations: } 2x = 4 \rightarrow x = 2 \rightarrow y = 10$$

$$\rightarrow x \times y = 20$$

8) Answer: D.

Formula for the Surface area of a cylinder is:

$$SA = 2\pi r^2 + 2\pi r h \rightarrow 168\pi = 2\pi r^2 + 2\pi r(8) \rightarrow r^2 + 8r -$$

$$84 = 0$$

$$(r + 14)(r - 6) = 0 \rightarrow r = 6 \quad or \quad r = -14\ (unacceptable)$$

9) Answer: E.

The slop of line A is: $m = \frac{y_2 - y_1}{x_2 - x_1} = \frac{4-3}{5-4} = 1$

Parallel lines have the same slope and only choice E ($y = x$) has

slope of 1.

10) Answer: D.

We know that, $\sqrt[n]{a^m} = a^{\frac{m}{n}}$ then:

$$\sqrt{y} = \sqrt{3^4} = 3^2 = 9 \rightarrow (3^4)^9 = 3^{36}$$

11) Answer: E.

$$\begin{cases} -\frac{x}{2} + \frac{y}{6} = 1 \\ -\frac{5y}{6} + 3x = 2 \end{cases} \rightarrow \text{multiply the top equation by 6 then:}$$

$$\begin{cases} -3x + y = 6 \\ -\frac{5y}{6} + 3x = 2 \end{cases} \rightarrow \text{add two equations}$$

$\frac{1}{6}y = 8 \rightarrow y = 48$, plug in the value of y into the first euation. $\rightarrow$

$$x = 14$$

12) Answer: B.

$$\text{average} = \frac{\text{sum of terms}}{\text{number of terms}}$$

The sum of the weight of all girls is: 16 × 65 = 1040 kg

The sum of the weight of all boys is: 34 × 67 = 2278 kg

The sum of the weight of all students is: 1040 + 2278 = 3318 kg

$$\text{average} = \frac{3318}{50} = 66.36$$

13) Answer: D.

Write the equation and solve for B:

0.80 A = 0.20 B, divide both sides by 0.20, then you will have

0.80/0.20 A = B, therefore:

B = 4 A, and B is 4 times of A or it's 400% of A.

14) Answer: B.

$$(x-4)^3 = 8 \rightarrow x - 4 = 2 \rightarrow x = 6$$
$$\rightarrow (x-5)(x-3) = (6-5)(6-3) = (1)(3) = 3$$

15) Answer: C.

Plug in the value of each option in the inequality.

A.	2	$(2-3)^2 + 1 > 3(2) - 1 \rightarrow 2 > 5$	No!
B.	5	$(5-3)^2 + 1 > 3(5) - 1 \rightarrow 5 > 14$	No!
C.	9	$(9-3)^2 + 1 > 3(9) - 1 \rightarrow 37 > 26$	Bingo!
D.	3	$(3-3)^2 + 1 > 3(3) - 1 \rightarrow 1 > 8$	No!
E.	4	$(4-3)^2 + 1 > 3(4) - 1 \rightarrow 2 > 11$	No!

16) Answer: B.

number of Mathematics books: $0.2 \times 700 = 140$

number of English books: $0.10 \times 700 = 70$

product of number of Mathematics and number of English books:

$140 \times 70 = 9,800$

17) Answer: B.

According to the chart, 50% of the books are in the Mathematics and Chemistry sections.

Therefore, there are 350 books in these two sections.

$0.50 \times 700 = 350$

$\gamma + \alpha = 350$, and $\gamma = \frac{2}{5}\alpha$

Replace γ by $\frac{2}{5}\alpha$ in the first equation.

$\gamma + \alpha = 350 \rightarrow \frac{2}{5}\alpha + \alpha = 350 \rightarrow \frac{7}{5}\alpha = 350$

(multiply both sides by $\frac{5}{7}$)

$\left(\frac{5}{7}\right)\frac{7}{5}\alpha = 350 \times \left(\frac{5}{7}\right) \rightarrow \alpha = \frac{350 \times 5}{7} = 250$

$\alpha = 250 \rightarrow \gamma = \frac{2}{5}\alpha \rightarrow \gamma = \frac{2}{5} \times 250 = 100$

There are 100 books in the Chemistry section.

18) Answer: D.

The angle α is: $0.2 \times 360 = 72°$

The angle β is: $0.15 \times 360 = 54°$

19) Answer: A.

We have: $(x + 3)(x + p) = x^2 + (3 + p)x + 3p \rightarrow 3 + p = 8 \rightarrow$

$p = 5 \ and \ r = 3p = 15$

20) Answer: A.

This question is a combination problem. The formula for

combination is: nCr $= \frac{n!}{r!(n-r)!}$

This formula is for the number of possible combinations of r

objects from a set of n objects.

Using the information in the question:

$$5C4= \frac{5!}{4!(5-4)!} = \frac{5\times4\times3\times2\times1}{4\times3\times2\times1\times(1)} = 5$$

GRE Quantitative Reasoning

Practice Tests 1

Section 2

1) Answer: B.

$\frac{1}{2^n} < \frac{1}{8} \rightarrow 2^{-n} < 2^{-3} \rightarrow -n < -3$, divide both sides by -1

$\rightarrow n > 3$

2) Answer: C.

Quantity A is: $\frac{2+6+x}{3} = 3 \rightarrow x = 1$

Quantity B is: $\frac{1+(1-2)+(1+1)+(1\times2)}{4} = 1$

3) Answer: C.

Simplify both quantities.

Quantity A: $(-3)^4 = (-3) \times (-3) \times (-3) \times (-3) = 81$

Quantity B: $3 \times 3 \times 3 \times 3 = 81$

The two quantities are equal.

4) Answer: D.

Simply change the fractions to decimals.

$\frac{3}{5} = 0.60$; $\frac{4}{6} = 0.66 \dots$; $\frac{5}{8} = 0.625$

As you can see, x lies between 0.60 and 0.666... and it can be 0.61 or 0.66. The first one is less than 0.625 and the second one is greater than 0.625.

The relationship cannot be determined from the information given.

5) Answer: A.

Simplify quantity B.

Quantity B: $(\frac{x}{5})^5 = \frac{x^5}{5^5}$

Since, the two quantities have the same numerator (x^5) and the denominator in quantity B is bigger ($5^5 > 5$), then the quantity A is greater.

6) Answer: A.

Use PEMDAS (order of operation):

Quantity A $= 10 + 8 \times (-3) - [4 + 32 \times 5] \div 4 = 10 + (-24) - [4 + 160] \div 4 = -14 - [164] \div 4 = -14 - 41 = -55$

Quantity B $= [6 \times (-24) + 8] - (-4) + [4 \times 5] \div 2 = [-144 + 8] + 4 + [20] \div 2 = [-136] + 4 + 10 = -136 + 14 = -122$

$-55 > -122$

7) Answer: C.

length of the rectangle is: $\frac{5}{4} \times 12 = 15$

perimeter of rectangle is: $2 \times (15 + 12) = 54$

8) Answer: D.

Th ratio of boy to girls is 7:4. Therefore, there are 7 boys out of 11 students. To find the answer, first divide the total number of students by 11, then multiply the result by 7.

$33 \div 11 = 3 \Rightarrow 3 \times 7 = 21$

There are 21 boys and 12 ($33 - 21$) girls. So, 14 more boys should be enrolled to make the ratio 1:1

9) Answer: A.

First, find the number.

Let x be the number. Write the equation and solve for x.

120 % of a number is 72, then:

$1.2 \times x = 72 \Rightarrow x = 72 \div 1.2 = 60$

90 % of 60 is: 0.9 × 60 = 54

10) Answer: D.

I. $|a| < 2 \rightarrow -2 < a < 2$

Multiply all sides by b. Since, $b > 0 \rightarrow -2b < ba < 2b$ (it is false)

II. Since, $-2 < a < 2, and\ a < 0 \rightarrow -a > a^2 > a$ (plug in $-\frac{1}{2}$, and

check!) (It's false)

III. $-2 < a < 2, multiply\ all\ sides\ by\ 2, then: -4 < 2a < 4$

Subtract 3 from all sides. Then:

$-4 - 3 < 2a - 3 < 2 - 3 \rightarrow -7 < 2a - 3 < 1$ (It is true!)

11) Answer: C.

Check each option provided:

A.　2　　$\dfrac{3+6+7+10+13}{5} = \dfrac{39}{5} = 7.8$

B.　3　　$\dfrac{2+6+7+10+13}{5} = \dfrac{38}{5} = 7.6$

C.　6　　$\dfrac{2+3+7+10+13}{5} = \dfrac{35}{5} = 7$

D.　10　　$\dfrac{2+3+6+7+13}{5} = \dfrac{30}{5} = 6.2$

E.　13　　$\dfrac{2+3+6+7+10}{5} = \dfrac{28}{5} = 5.6$

12) Answer: B.

To find the discount, multiply the number by (100% − rate of discount).

Therefore, for the first discount we get: (D) (100% − 40%) = (D) (0.60) = 0.60 D

For increase of 10 %: (0.60 D) (100% + 10%) = (0.60 D) (1.10) = 0.66 D = 66% of D

13) Answer: D.

Let x be the length of AB, then:

$$10 = \frac{x \times 4}{2} \rightarrow x = 5$$

The length of AC $= \sqrt{5^2 + 12^2} = \sqrt{169} = 13$

The perimeter of $\Delta ABC = 5 + 12 + 13 = 30$

14) Answer: D.

Since line l is parallel to x-axis, therefore the slope of l is equal to 0 and the value of y is the same as the value of y in the point (-4, 5). Therefore, y-intercept is 5.

15) Answer: B.

$$|x - 2x - 6 + 8| = 3$$
$$\rightarrow |-x + 2| = 3 \rightarrow -x + 2 = 3 \; or - x + 2 = -3$$
$$\rightarrow x = -1 \; or \; x = 5$$

The product of all possible values of x = $(-1) \times 5 = -5$

16) Answer: D.

First find the number of pants sold in each month.

January: 110, February: 88, March: 90, April: 70, May: 85, June: 65

Check each option provided.

A. There is a decrease from January to February

B. February and March, $\left(\frac{90-88}{90}\right) \times 100 = \frac{2}{90} \times 100 = 2.22\%$

C. There is a decrease from March to April

D. April and May: there is an increase from April to May

$\left(\frac{84-70}{70}\right) \times 100 = \frac{14}{70} \times 100 = 20\%$

E. There is a decrease from May to June.

17) Answer: C.

First, order the number of shirts sold each month:

$130, 140, 144, 150, 160, 170$

mean is: $\frac{130+140+144+150+160+170}{6} = \frac{894}{6} = 149$

Put the number of shoes sold per month in order:

$20, 25, 25, 35, 35, 40$; median is: $\frac{25+35}{2} = 30$

18) Answer: B.

The ratio of number of pants to number of shoes in May equals $\frac{84}{25}$.

Five-seventeenth of this ratio is $\left(\frac{5}{12}\right)\left(\frac{84}{25}\right)$. Now, let x be the

number of shoes needed to be added in April.

$\frac{70}{20+x} = \left(\frac{5}{12}\right)\left(\frac{84}{25}\right) \rightarrow \frac{70}{20+x} = \frac{420}{300} = 1.4 \rightarrow 70 = 1.4(20+x) \rightarrow 70 =$

$28 + 1.4x \rightarrow 1.4x = 42 \rightarrow x = 30$

19) Answer: D.

The rectangle is inscribed in a circle. Therefore, the diagonal of the

rectangle is the diameter of the circle.

Use Pythagorean theorem to solve for the diagonal of the rectangle.

$a^2 + b^2 = c^2$

$8^2 + 15^2 = c^2 \rightarrow 64 + 225 =$

$c^2 \rightarrow 289 = c^2 \rightarrow c = 17$

The diameter of the circle is 17.

Therefore, the circumference of

the circle is:

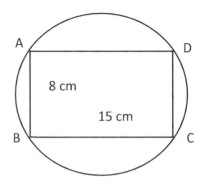

$C = \pi d = \pi \times 17 = 17\pi$

20) Answer: D.

The area of ΔBED is 12, then: $\dfrac{6 \times AB}{2} = 12 \rightarrow 6 \times AB = 24 \rightarrow AB = 4$

The area of ΔBDF is 16, then: $\dfrac{4 \times BC}{2} = 16 \rightarrow 4 \times BC = 32 \rightarrow BC = 8$

The perimeter of the rectangle is = $2 \times (8 + 4) = 24$

Answers and Explanations

GRE Quantitative Reasoning

Practice Tests 2

Section 1

1) Answer: B.

Since, x is a positive integer greater than 1, then the minimum value of $\sqrt{x}$ is greater than 1.

2) Answer: B.

$$(x - y)^2 = (x - y)(x - y) = x^2 - 2xy + y^2 \rightarrow \text{Since } y^2 > 0$$
$$\rightarrow x^2 - 2xy + y^2 > x^2 - 2xy$$

3) Answer: B.

Use factoring method to solve for x in the equation.

$$x^2 - 4x - 12 = 0 \rightarrow (x - 6)(x + 2) = 0$$

Then: $(x - 6) = 0 \rightarrow x = 6$

Or $(x + 2) = 0 \rightarrow x = -2$

Both values of x are less than 6. So, quantity B is greater

4) Answer: B.

Solve for p and q in the equation.

$(p, 0): y = \frac{2}{3}x + 14 \rightarrow 0 = \frac{2}{3}p + 14$; Solve for p in the equation.

$0 = \frac{2}{3}p + 14 \rightarrow \frac{2}{3}p = -14 \rightarrow p = (-14) \times \left(\frac{3}{2}\right) = -21$

$(0, q): y = \frac{2}{3}x + 14 \rightarrow q = \frac{2}{3}(0) + 14 \rightarrow q = 14 \Longrightarrow q > p$

5) Answer: D.

Let's choose some values for x and y.

$x = 1$, $y = 0.5 \rightarrow (A = 1.5) > (B = 0.5)$ and if $x = 1$ and $y = -0.5 \rightarrow B > A$

6) Answer: C.

The loan is $17,000 and its interest is $1,530. Since the interest is for 2 years. Therefore, the simple interest rate (p) per year is $765.

Then:

interest rate$= \dfrac{interest\ amount}{loan} \times 100 \rightarrow p = \dfrac{765}{17000} \times 100 = 4.5$

7) Answer: A.

The relationship among all sides of special right triangle

$30° - 60° - 90°$ is provided in this triangle:

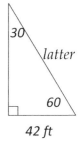

In this triangle, the opposite side of $30°$ angle is half of the hypotenuse.

Draw the shape of this question.

The latter is the hypotenuse. Therefore, the latter is 84 feet.

8) Answer: C.

average (mean) $= \dfrac{\text{sum of terms}}{\text{number of terms}} \Rightarrow 77 = \dfrac{\text{sum of terms}}{60} \Rightarrow$ sum $= 77 \times$

60 = 4620

The difference of 64 and 46 is 18. Therefore, 18 should be subtracted from the sum, $4620 - 18 = 4602$

mean $= \dfrac{\text{sum of terms}}{\text{number of terms}} \Rightarrow$ mean $= \dfrac{4602}{60} = 76.7$

9) Answer: D.

To get a sum of 6 or 4 for two dice, we should get 1 and 3, 2 and 2, or 4 and 2, 3 and 3, and 5 and 1. Therefore, there are 8 options. Since, we have 6 × 6 = 36 total options, the probability of getting a sum of 6 or 4 is 8 out of 36 or $\frac{8}{36} = \frac{2}{9}$.

10) Answer: C.

Since, $64 = 2^4$

Then: $(2^{6x})(64) = 2^{2y} \rightarrow (2^{6x})(2^4) = 2^{2y}$

Use exponent "product rule": $x^n \times x^m = x^{n+m}$

$$(2^{6x})(2^4) = 2^{2y} \rightarrow (2^{6x+4}) = 2^{2y}$$

The bases are the same. Therefore, the powers must be equal.

$$6x + 4 = 2y$$

Divide both sides of the equation by 2: $6x + 4 = 2y \rightarrow 3x + 2 = y$

11) Answer: E.

Th ratio of boy to girls is 2:4. Therefore, there are 2 boys out of 6 students. To find the answer, first divide the total number of students by 6, then multiply the result by 2.

600 ÷ 6 = 100 ⇒ 100 × 2 = 200

12) Answer: A.

Area of the triangle is: $\frac{1}{2} AD \times BC$ and AD is perpendicular to BC.

Triangle ADC is a $30° - 60° - 90°$ right triangle. The relationship among all sides of right triangle $30° - 60° - 90°$ is provided in the following triangle:

In this triangle, the opposite side of 30° angle is half of the hypotenuse. And the opposite side of 60° is opposite of 30° × $\sqrt{3}$

CD = 5, then AD = 5 × $\sqrt{3}$

Area of the triangle ABC is: $\frac{1}{2} AD \times BC = \frac{1}{2} 5\sqrt{3} \times 10 = 25\sqrt{3}$

13) Answer: E.

$$0.9x = (0.3) \times 30 \to x = 10 \to (x + 3)^2 = (13)^2 = 169$$

14) Answer: C.

The width of the rectangle is twice its length. Let x be the length.

Then, $width = 2x$

Perimeter of the rectangle is 2 (width + length) = $2(2x + x) = 120$

$\Rightarrow 6x = 120 \Rightarrow x = 20$

Length of the rectangle is 20 meters.

15) Answer: C.

Solving Systems of Equations by Elimination

Multiply the first equation by (−2), then add it to the second equation.

$$\begin{array}{l} -3(2x + 5y = 11) \\ \underline{6x + 3y = -3} \end{array} \Rightarrow \begin{array}{l} -6x - 15y = -33 \\ 6x + 3y = -3 \end{array} \Rightarrow -12y = -36$$

$\Rightarrow y = 3$

Plug in the value of y into one of the equations and solve for x.

$$2x + 5(3) = 11 \Rightarrow 2x + 15 = 11 \Rightarrow 2x = -4 \Rightarrow x = -2$$

16) Answer: C.

Let's find the mean (average), mode and median of the number of cities for each type of pollution.

Number of cities for each type of pollution: 6, 3, 4, 9, 8

$$average\ (mean) = \frac{sum\ of\ terms}{number\ of\ terms} = \frac{6+3+4+9+8}{5} = \frac{30}{5} = 6$$

Median is the number in the middle. To find median, first list numbers in order from smallest to largest: 3, 4, 6, 8, 9

Median of the data is 6.

Mode is the number which appears most often in a set of numbers. Therefore, there is no mode in the set of numbers.

Median = Mean, then, $a=c$

17) Answer: B.

Let the number of cities should be added to type of pollutions C be x. Then: $\frac{x+3}{8} = 0.750 \rightarrow x + 3 = 8 \times 0.750 \rightarrow x + 3 = 6 \rightarrow x = 3$

18) Answer: D.

Four years ago, Amy was x times as old as Mike. Mike is 8 years now. Therefore, 4 years ago Mike was 4 years old.

Four years ago, Amy was: $A = 4 \times x = 4x$

Now Amy is: $A = 4x + 4$

19) Answer: D.

x and z are colinear. y and $6x$ are colinear. Therefore,

$x + z = y + 6x,\ subtract\ x\ from\ both\ sides, then, z = y + 5x$

20) Answer: E.

$$average = \frac{sum\ of\ terms}{number\ of\ terms} \Rightarrow (average\ of\ 6\ numbers)\ 14$$

$$= \frac{sum\ of\ numbers}{6} \Rightarrow sum\ of\ 6\ numbers\ is\ 14 \times 6 = 84$$

(average of 4 numbers) $10 = \frac{\text{sum of numbers}}{4} \Rightarrow$ sum of 4 numbers is

$10 \times 4 = 40$

sum of 6 numbers − sum of 4 numbers = sum of 2 numbers

$84 - 40 = 44$

average of 2 numbers $= \frac{44}{2} = 22$

GRE Quantitative Reasoning

Practice Tests 2

Section 2

1) Answer: D.

Choose different values for x and find the value of quantity A and quantity B.

$x = 1$, then: Quantity A: $x^{20} = 1^{20} = 1$

Quantity B: $x^{30} = 1^{30} = 1$

The two quantities are equal.

$x = 2$, then: Quantity A: $x^{20} = 2^{20}$

Quantity B: $x^{30} = 2^{30}$; Quantity B is greater.

Therefore, the relationship cannot be determined from the information given.

2) Answer: C.

Use exponent "product rule": $x^n \times x^m = x^{n+m}$

Quantity A: $(1.88)^3 (1.88)^7 = (1.88)^{3+7} = (1.88)^{10}$

Quantity B: $(1.88)^{10}$

The two quantities are equal.

3) Answer: C.

Area of a circle $= \pi r^2 \rightarrow 81 = \pi r^2 \rightarrow r^2 = \frac{81}{\pi} \rightarrow r = \frac{9}{\sqrt{\pi}}$

4) Answer: A.

$\frac{x+4}{4} = \frac{x}{4} + 1$

$$\frac{x^2-25}{x^2-5x} = \frac{(x-5)(x+5)}{x(x-5)} = \frac{x+5}{x} = 1 + \frac{5}{x}$$

Since, $\frac{x}{4} > \frac{5}{x}$ for the values of $5 < x < 9 \rightarrow$ Quantity A > Quantity B

5) Answer: A.

Volume of a right cylinder = $\pi r^2 h \rightarrow 75\pi = \pi r^2 h = \pi(2)^2 h \rightarrow$

$h = 18.75$

6) The answer is 9.

Set A: {9, 5, 12, 8, 6, x, y} ; Set B: {5, 8, x, y}

The average of the 4 numbers in Set B is 9. Therefore:

$\frac{5+8+x+y}{4} = 9$, multiply both sides of the equation by 4.

$\rightarrow 13 + x + y = 36 \rightarrow x + y = 23$

Let's find the average of the 6 numbers in Set A when the sum of x

and y is 23, $\frac{9+5+12+8+6+x+y}{7} = \frac{40+(x+y)}{7} = \frac{40+23}{7} = 9$

7) Answer: D.

Method 1: Solve for x.

$(x^2 + x)(x - 4) = 6x \rightarrow x^3 - 3x^2 - 4x = 6x \rightarrow x(x^2 - 3x -$

$10) = 0 \rightarrow x(x + 2)(x - 5) = 0 \rightarrow x = 0 \ or \ x = -2 \ or \ x = 5$

Method 2: Plugin the options and check.

A. 0 $\qquad (0^2 + 0)(0 - 4) = -10(0) \rightarrow 0 = 0!$ It works!

B. 0, $3 - \sqrt{3}, \sqrt{3} + 3 \qquad \left((3 - \sqrt{3})^2 + (\sqrt{3} - 3)\right)(\sqrt{3} - 3 - 4) =$

$-6(\sqrt{3} - 3) \rightarrow (12 - \sqrt{3})(\sqrt{3} - 7) = -6\sqrt{3} + 18 \rightarrow 5\sqrt{3} - 84 \neq$

$-6\sqrt{3} + 18$, not a solution!

C. 0, -3, -5 $((-3)^2 - 3)(-3 - 4) = -6(-3) \rightarrow -42 \neq 18!$ not a

solution!

D. 0, 2, -5 $((5)^2 + 5)(5 - 4) = 6(5) \rightarrow 30 = 30!$, Bingo!

$((-2)^2 - 2)(-2 - 4) = -6(-2) \rightarrow -12 = -12!$ Bingo!

E. No solution

8) Answer: B.

$$a = b - 0.4b = 0.6b \rightarrow \frac{a}{b} = \frac{0.6b}{b} = 0.6 \rightarrow \left(\frac{a}{b}\right)^2 = (0.6)^2 = 0.36$$

9) Answer: C.

The population of the city is increased by 25% and 40%. 25%

increase changes the population to 125% of original population.

For the second increase, multiply the result by 140%.

(1.25) × (1.40) = 1.75 = 175%

75 percent of the population is increased after two years.

10) Answer: D.

x and z are colinear. y and $6x$ are colinear. Therefore,

$x + z = y + 6x$, subtract x from both sides, then, $z = y + 5x$

11) Answer: A.

Since the outcomes are mutually exclusive. Then, the sum of

probabilities of all outcomes equals to 1.

Therefore: $n + \dfrac{n}{2} + \dfrac{3n}{4} = 1$

Find a common denominator and solve for n.

$$n + \frac{n}{2} + \frac{3n}{4} = 1 \rightarrow \frac{4n}{4} + \frac{2n}{4} + \frac{3n}{4} = 1 \rightarrow \frac{9n}{4} = 1 \rightarrow 9n = 4 \rightarrow n = \frac{4}{9}$$

12) Answer: C.

Let x be the smallest number. Then, these are the numbers:

$x, x + 1, x + 2, x + 3, x + 4$

$$\text{average} = \frac{\text{sum of terms}}{\text{number of terms}} \Rightarrow 36 = \frac{x+(x+1)+(x+2)+(x+3)+(x+4)}{5}$$

$$\Rightarrow 36 = \frac{5x+10}{5} \Rightarrow 180 = 5x + 10 \Rightarrow 170 = 5x \Rightarrow x = 34$$

13) Answer: C.

4% of the volume of the solution is alcohol. Let x be the volume of the solution.

Then: 4% of x = 36 ml $\Rightarrow 0.04\, x = 36 \Rightarrow x = 36 \div 0.04 = 800$

14) Answer: C.

Solve for the sum of five numbers.

$$\text{average} = \frac{\text{sum of terms}}{\text{number of terms}} \Rightarrow 22 = \frac{\text{sum of 5 numbers}}{5} \Rightarrow \text{sum of 5}$$

numbers = 22 × 5 = 110

The sum of 5 numbers is 110. If a sixth number 52 is added, then the sum of 6 numbers is: 110 + 52 = 162

$$\text{average} = \frac{\text{sum of terms}}{\text{number of terms}} = \frac{162}{6} = 27$$

15) Answer: B, C, and F.

n is even. Plug in an even number for n and check the options.

Let's choose 2 for n. Then:

A.	$n + 11$	$2 + 11 = 13$	Odd
B.	$n^2 + 2(n + 1)$	$2^2 + 2(2 + 1) = 4 + 2(3) = 10$	Even
C.	$7n$	$7 \times 2 = 10$	Even
D.	$3n^2 + 5n$	$3(2)^2 + 5(2) = 3 \times 4 + 10 = 17$	Odd
E.	$n^3 + 3n + 1$	$2^3 + 3(2) + 1 = 8 + 6 + 1 = 15$	Odd
F.	$4(n + 3)$	$4(2 + 3) = 20$	Even

16) **Answer: D.**

Percentage of women in city C $= \frac{700}{1365} \times 100 = 51.28\%$

Percentage of men in city B $= \frac{300}{591} \times 100 = 50.76\%$

Percentage of men in city A to percentage of women in city C: $\frac{51.28}{50.76} = 1.01$

17) **Answer: C.**

Ratio of women to men in city A: $\frac{570}{600}$=0.95

Ratio of women to men in city B: $\frac{291}{300}$=0.97

Ratio of women to men in city C: $\frac{665}{700}$=0.95

Ratio of women to men in city D: $\frac{528}{550}$=0.96

18) **Answer: B.**

Let the number of women should be added to city D be x, then:

$\frac{528 + x}{550} = 1.3 \rightarrow 528 + x = 550 \times 1.3 = 715 \rightarrow x = 187$

19) **Answer: E.**

Based on triangle similarity theorem: $\frac{a}{a+b} = \frac{c}{3} \rightarrow c = \frac{3a}{a+b} = \frac{3\sqrt{2}}{3\sqrt{2}} = 1$

$\rightarrow$ area of shaded region is: $\left(\frac{c+3}{2}\right)(b) = \frac{4}{2} \times 2\sqrt{2} = 4\sqrt{2}$

20) **Answer: C.**

The speed of car A is 68 mph and the speed of car B is 82 mph. When both cars drive in a straight line toward each other, the distance between the cars decreases at the rate of 150 miles per hour: 68 + 82 = 150

40 minutes is two third of an hour. Therefore, they will be 100 miles apart 40 minutes before they meet ($\frac{2}{3} \times 150 = 100$)

"End"